Also by Dow Tippett

Submission: The Choice to Love,
The Freedom to Live, The Power to Lead
Devotions from the Dojo

7 DAILY CHOICES

a leadership fable

HOW TO CREATE, BUILD, AND SUSTAIN
A THRIVING LIFE WITH OTHERS

DOW TIPPETT

Published by Author Academy Elite

P.O. Box 43, Powell, OH 43035

www.AuthorAcademyElite.com

ISBN

Paperback: 978-1-64085-438-3

Hardback: 978-1-64085-439-0

Ebook: 978-1-64085-440-6

Library of Congress Control Number (LCCN): 2018957227

For my wife and girls who make my life worth living. And for Jesus Christ who became one of us that we might follow "in his steps."

CONTENTS

BEDROCK

Dear George: —
Remember _no_ man
is a failure who has
friends.

Thanks for the wings!
Love
Clarence

INTRODUCTION:
THE MAN IN CONFLICT

As the rain fell hard on the window of the local diner, Donny stared aimlessly across the parking lot at nothing in the distance. His mind returned to his eggs and bacon and he began to eat but again found himself staring at the same nothing.

"Distracted men often go hungry," Donny's head shot up, and he saw Scott, a business man from church who Donny had always respected but wondered if he wasn't a little too happy.

"Hi, Scott. Just doing a lot of thinking."

"Well, that's dangerous. You alone?"

Donny's first thought was "I was until you showed up," then, "Talking about anything might not be a bad distraction." So, he said, "Yeah, unless you join me."

As Scott sat down, Donny tried to put away the fight he'd had with Amanda last night and prepared to just relax for a minute.

"How's Amanda?" Scott asked.

Donny suddenly wondered if Scott was a mind reader, but just as he was going to answer with a pat, "She's fine,"

Sarah, the morning waitress, stepped to the table. "Hey Scott, are you having your number one?"

"No, Sarah, I'm still trying to lose these 15 pounds."

"Oh yeah, so . . ."

"Three eggs over-easy, and some bacon, please, no carbs."

"Coffee?"

"Yes, please."

While all this happened, Donny's answer was stirring in his head. Could he, should he spill everything to Scott? He really didn't know Scott that well. They had talked at church, his girls were regular help in the nursery, and his kids loved them. They had had a few deep conversations over the Bible and Donny's work, but Scott didn't know anything close to this.

As Sarah walked away, Scott turned back and just stared, Donny sat quietly, running the debate in his head. Scott simply looked Donny in the eye and waited. The moments seemed to drag out in slow motion, and the discomfort was unbearable. Then to his own surprise, Donny said, "Well, we had a pretty big fight last night. In fact, that's what I was sitting here mulling over when you came in. To be honest, Scott, I don't know what happened. We sat down after the kids were in bed and started a conversation about money and vacation plans, and by the end of the night she was in bed crying, and I was laying there staring at the ceiling wondering if I was ever going to be able to have a deep discussion with her without being goaded into a fight."

"Coffee?" Sarah had returned and broke the crazed stream of consciousness that had just flowed from Donny, but it did feel good to tell someone.

After, Sarah left, Donny tried not to fume, as he waited for Scott's platitudes to flow. Instead, Scott simply said, "It does seem like a fight is always looming, doesn't it?" and fell silent again.

"Well, not all the time," Donny replied, "but lately, and you know it's not just at home either. When I am at work it seems like my boss is looking for the smallest things to point out. Stuff that really doesn't matter, but he wants it a specific way. I can't own anything, because he won't let go. And if it's not my boss, it's an employee who doesn't want to follow simple procedure that allows us to be more productive. Everywhere I turn, it seems someone is itching for a fight."

"Wow, that's got to be tough," Scott answered.

"It is, and I'm tired."

Scott and Donny were quiet for moment as Sarah dropped off Scott's food and pleasantries were exchanged.

When Sarah walked away Scott asked, "Did you know I teach martial arts?"

"This conversation just took a strange turn," Donny thought, but said, "How's that going?"

"Oh, business is booming, more than I can really handle right now. But the reason I bring it up is that I have learned so much about how to handle conflict in relationships from the training we do in the dojo. It seems like you're struggling with a lot of conflict, and maybe martial arts can help."

"Really, I never would have guessed karate could help. Amanda has been saying that I need to find a hobby, and I used to love all the karate movies back in the day. What time are classes?"

"Well for you, classes are at 6 pm on Tuesday or Thursday."

"How much is it?"

"Well, we have a whole scale of pricing, but you should drop in and check it out, the first class is always free."

"Can I bring the girls?"

"Absolutely, I love teaching families, and we do special pricing when there's more than two family members attending."

Sarah stepped back up to fill the coffee one more time, and Scott turned to his food. Then finishing a bite quickly, he said, "If you want to go back to sharing your struggles, I am ready to listen." Donny wasn't sure if he should share or not. Did he know Scott well enough?

Donny decided to move on. "Actually, Scott, it just felt good to get it out. I think I will be okay for now."

"Okay, so did you hear about the food plant going in on Evan's Drive?"

From there the conversation drifted from one innocuous topic to the other, until Donny was ready to get on with his day. As they stood to leave, Scott said, "Thanks for letting me share breakfast with you, we should do it again."

"No, I should thank *you*," said Donny, "You really helped get the day started in a positive direction instead of the depression I was facing, and I would love to do it again."

"Great!" said Scott, "Here is a card, if you want to show up Tuesday, and maybe we could schedule now to do this again next Thursday."

"Done."

The two men shook hands and headed out. Donny didn't know what had happened, but he had a sense that his world shifted.

CREATE

CHOOSE VULNERABILITY

As Donny pulled into the garage Tuesday evening, he was in pretty good spirits. No major conflicts had arisen at work, and he and Amanda had been so busy running the girls on Saturday that there really wasn't time to fight. Sunday had been restful. Yesterday he had found himself in a conversation with a coworker with whom he had had nothing but conflict, but as they talked, he began to realize that John had just grown up hard. His brash nature was probably a great improvement, and Donny began to feel grace for John.

When Donny walked in the house, it was obvious something was wrong. Laynie, Donny's youngest, was stomping upstairs, and Amanda was upset.

"What's wrong?" Donny asked.

"She doesn't want to go!" Amanda all but shouted.

"To go where?" Donny asked again, just trying to figure out how to fix whatever was going to ruin a perfectly good day.

"Karate. Didn't you want to take them to karate?"

"Oh yeah, that's tonight." Donny had forgotten in his reveling about the other things happening. "Ok, I'll talk to her."

Donny went upstairs and found Laynie lying face down on her bed crying. "Hey, girlie," He said gently, "what's up?"

"I don't want to wear those pants," Laynie pointed to a pair of sweat pants across the room.

"Ok, sweetie," Donny answered, realizing this was about way more than pants. "What else can you wear?"

"Nothing, everything looks stupid. Karate's stupid."

"Wow, you seemed so excited on Friday, when we talked about going, and I was excited to spend time with you and Katie." Donny wasn't sure if he should just give up, but the idea of being able to do something with his girls that might bond them together appealed to a deep need as a father.

Laynie calming down said, "Cindy said karate is for boys!"

"Really," Donny responded, truly shocked, and ready to give Cindy a reason to take karate, "I happen to know all of Sensei Scott's girls have taken karate. You know Alex from church who helps in your class? I think she might even help teach.

What if we go tonight and try it, then if you don't like it, we won't go back?"

Laynie leaned into her dad's chest, and he gave her a squeeze, feeling the joy of being the good dad. "Now why don't you get something comfortable on and we'll go have fun okay?"

"Okay."

"I love you," Donny said as he kissed her on the head.

Donny headed down stairs and saw Katie sitting on the couch, "Are you ready to try this?"

"I'm nervous, but sure, why not?" Katie answered. Then in the kitchen, where Amanda was washing dishes, Scott wrapped his arms around her, kissed her cheek, and asked hopefully, "You sure, you don't want to come?"

Without looking up Amanda answered softly, "No, you and the girls have fun. I'll have dinner ready when you get home."

Scott knew things weren't okay, but he also knew he needed to be kind, especially right now, when Amanda had been dealing with an unreasonable child. Laynie came bounding down the stairs in a bright green t-shirt and the same sweat pants she had just called stupid. Amanda looked at her, then at Scott, then went back to washing dishes without a word.

When they arrived at The Good Fight Dojo, the first person to greet them was Alex, and Donny breathed a sigh of relief as Laynie rushed to give her a hug.

"Hey, girls, my dad said you might come tonight. I am so glad to see you," Alex was such a nice girl. Dependable and strong, and beautiful. If his girls could have her for a mentor, they would probably be alright.

"Cindy said karate was for boys!" Laynie blurted out.

Donny held his breath, but was relieved when Alex didn't flinch, "Well, you tell Cindy, that some people think the name Alex is for boys too, but I AM NOT A BOY." Alex emphasized each word with pride and strength. Then in a softer tone, "Come see."

Alex took Laynie and Katie by the hand and led them into the studio where Scott was teaching a group of children, all younger than Laynie, boys and girls. Scott was sitting on the floor finishing up the class.

When the class was over, Scott helped the kids get homework and made his way over to Donny. Other black belts and students were milling around stretching getting into uniform, and Donny suddenly felt completely out of place. Two other Dads were getting ready, but they clearly knew what was happening, while Donny was completely lost.

Reaching out to shake Donny's hand, Scott said, "I am so glad you could make it."

"Yeah," said Donny, "I wasn't sure. We had a little issue with Laynie, but we're here."

"Great." Turning to one of the other adults with a black belt, Scott said, "Jeff, this is Donny. He and his girls are checking us out."

Jeff reached out a hand, "Good to meet you, Donny. You're gonna love it. My son and I have been here for almost five years now. Best thing we ever did together."

"Jeff, could you get class started in a few minutes while I get Donny set up?" Scott asked.

"No problem, Sensei." Jeff said and moved on.

Then Scott turned to Alex, "You got them?" asking about Laynie and Katie. Alex shot him a thumbs-up.

Donny felt the pressure lift off his shoulders knowing the girls were going to be okay.

"So, I don't want to take too long, so you can jump in. We have all our new students line up in the back. I'm sure you will catch on quick. I'll answer any questions when we're done."

A little uncertain again, Donny let out, "I hope I don't look stupid." "Everyone starts from scratch," Scott said with a laugh.

"Okay, here we go." Donny stepped into line with his girls behind about 12 other students with different colored belts. He didn't know what the colors meant, but they were obviously grouped in order.

Scott stepped to the front of the class, and said, "Let's pray.

Father, tonight we ask that you keep us safe as we train. Please, help us to learn quickly and be sharp of mind. Mostly, Lord, we ask that what we learn tonight will help us to become more like Jesus in every part of our life. Amen."

Donny wasn't expecting class to start with prayer but was glad to see Jesus being honored.

"Feet together!" Scott continued. Everyone stood at attention. "Bow!" Everyone bowed, Donny glanced sideways at his girls joining the group and bowed as well.

As the training began, Donny found himself a little out of place several times as everything was new. They spent most of their time working on what Scott called a parry block. As he demonstrated the block, it was simply one hand up, like a vertical karate chop, then you turned sideways to avoid a punch. Scott then demonstrated with Jeff, and it looked like Jeff had really tried to punch Scott, but Scott had avoided the strike easily. Donny was impressed.

"Remember," Scott said, "We don't move our hand during this block. We turn our hips. Where is our power?"

"In our hips!" the whole class said in unison as if from a military chant.

"Right," Scott spoke loud enough for everyone to here, not mean like a drill sergeant, but strong like one. "The power is in the hips. If my center is strong, everything is strong. When I depend on the power in my center, I can overcome any attack."

Then in a quieter tone, "Who's in our center?"

A little girl, not much older than Laynie, raised her hand, and said, "Jesus."

Smiling at her Scott said, "Right, Izzy. Jesus is our power, when we keep Him in the center. No schemes of our enemy will overtake us."

The class moved on, but Donny considered Scott's thought as they moved through different drills and activities. "If Jesus is my center, why am I struggling?" he thought. When they started to learn what Scott called "kata," Donny found himself once again feeling more uncoordinated than he had in a long time. Donny had been an athlete most of his life, but this was totally different. Nothing felt normal, and he really didn't like not being good at something. Worse still, Katie took to it like a fish in the ocean. Suddenly, though, Donny felt proud and safe. Katie at least was going to enjoy this.

"Yame! Shugo!" Scott called out Japanese commands that meant, "Stop and line up." Then he gave the command that everyone was to sit.

"Today we focused on blocking. Every time we do a kata we start with a block. Today we really spent time on a Parry Block. When we are confronted by someone who appears to be attacking us, the first thing I want you to do is put your hands up.

Now, what does it look like I am doing when I put my hands up?" "Surrendering," said one student Donny hadn't met.

"Right, the first step in self-defense is to surrender. Put your hands up. Now an attacker is going to think we are an easy target and he will relax, but the reality is we are putting ourselves in a position to have influence. Instead of choosing what looks like a protective position, we choose a vulnerable one, and we become stronger.

This is also true when we face conflict with others. When someone hurts our feelings, or seems to be attacking us with words, we need to choose a vulnerable position. We might be able to exert influence over those who are weaker than us when we fight back, but when we choose to be vulnerable we can exert positive influence to bring peace over anyone.

One of the best ways to be vulnerable is to offer two words, 'I'm sorry.'

So often when we feel hurt, we also did something to make the other person feel hurt. We may not be responsible for the whole situation, but we can apologize for what is our part. Because, let's be honest, most of us are never going to meet a thug on the street, but we all have conflict with people, and it is usually someone we live with, someone we love.

So, next time your sister hurts your feelings, instead of getting mad back, what if you choose to be vulnerable.

Where is the power in the parry block?" "Our hips." the class said.

"And who is the power in our center that let's vulnerability bring peace?"

"Jesus," Donny noticed as he quietly repeated that his girls had answered too. This was so cool.

When they walked back in the house, Amanda was sitting on the couch reading a book. Laynie ran straight to her mom and said, "Mommy, Alex was there, and she helped us all night. She said to tell Cindy, that people think Alex is a boy's name, but she is NOT A BOY!" Laynie used the same emphasis that Alex had used. Then she looked at her mom and said, "And mommy, Sensei Scott said that when we have our feelings hurt, we sometimes hurt other people, and we should say we're sorry."

"Did he?" Amanda said, as she glanced at Donny, then back at Laynie with a smile.

"Mommy, I'm sorry." Laynie wrapped her arms around Amanda's neck and and squeezed. Donny thought he saw Amanda tear up.

When class had ended, Scott had taken a few minutes to give Donny all the details of payment, uniforms, fighting gear, etc., and had spent time making sure the girls had fun. Then he confirmed plans for breakfast at the diner on Thursday.

"Thanks, for the lesson at the end," Donny said.

Scott looked Donny directly in the eyes, "Donny, what we do here is train Christian leaders, and today's lesson will get repeated a lot, the moment we are willing to choose vulnerability is the moment we gain influence to bring peace to the world." Donny felt like God was speaking to his soul. Scott turned to his notes, and the pressure released. "So, if you make it back next week, you can pay for the girls?"

Donny was overwhelmed by the grace. Fifteen dollars a class was a bargain if every week brought this much insight.

On Thursday morning, Donny arrived at the diner a few minutes late and saw Scott reading on his phone and sipping coffee.

"Sorry, I am late."

"Way to be vulnerable, my friend." Scott smiled back clearly not bothered.

Sarah came and took both men's order and they settled in. "So, the girls enjoyed class?" Scott asked.

"Yeah, I told you Laynie had issues before we came." Donny said, making sure Scott remembered. Scott sat with listening eyes. "Well, after your lesson, she went straight home and apologized to Amanda."

"Cool," Scott responded, "I am so glad. Someone is listening. What about you?"

"What do you mean?" Donny asked, not sure what to think of Scott's question. The truth was he had enjoyed the class, and even felt that God was working on his heart, but surely Scott didn't expect him to go straight home and apologize to Amanda. Their issues were bigger than a fight over pants and solving them wasn't as simple as an apology. Then he thought, maybe Scott was just asking if he enjoyed class.

He went with the easy answer, "Yeah, I liked it."

"Great," Scott replied with enthusiasm. "How are things with Amanda?"

"Okay," Donny answered. At least it wasn't a complete lie. They hadn't fought again since last week, but the distance between them was obvious.

"Awesome," Scott said, "Because usually things don't go from bad and fighting all the time to good again in just a week. God must have done a miracle." Donny noted the sarcasm . . . and brilliance of Scott's response. He had just given Donny the chance to get out gracefully and called him on the carpet in the same breath. This guy was good.

"Well, we haven't fought since last Thursday." Donny shared exact truth, if not the whole truth.

"Good, but are you finding your way back to wholeness?" Scott asked. Then waited.

"No," Donny finally admitted. "We aren't avoiding each other really, but we just don't say anything significant. I think if we did, we would probably fight again." Donny couldn't decide if he was embarrassed or relieved for sharing.

Scott fixed his gaze on Donny again, "Donny, if you want to get straight, you have to be straight. We don't have time to play games with each other, so let me be very clear. I haven't taken the time to let you know me well enough to trust me with stuff that could get you in trouble, but I have been probing like we've been friends for years. I am sorry. I was wrong. Will you forgive me?"

"Sure," Donny said, realizing he wasn't even offended.

"Thank you, and Donny, if I ever probe where you aren't comfortable, or you see me doing the same thing to someone else, I give you permission to hold me accountable, so that I don't cause unnecessary discomfort."

"Okay, thanks." Again, Donny wasn't sure what was happening. He was the one who had held back the truth. He was the one who was wasting time. If this guy had answers, Donny should not hide behind his pride. He should be opening himself up to whatever Scott can teach him.

"Donny, is there anything else I've done to hurt our relationship that I need to apologize for?"

"No," Donny said, "But I'm sorry, I was holding back. You've never given me any reason to doubt your genuine care, and I still didn't trust you."

"I didn't give you time," Scott said, seeming genuinely repentant. For a moment, Donny sat quiet, and Sarah brought breakfast.

Scott asked if he could pray. "Father, I thank you for Donny. Thank you for our new budding friendship. Help us to help each other become more like your Son. Thank you for this food and the work you will do in us today. Amen."

As Donny sat again in awe of the man across from him, the tumblers fell. Almost shouting he blurted out, "Vulnerability!"

Scott just smiled.

"You just played me," Donny said half laughing.

Scott got dead serious, "Oh no, Donny, I wasn't playing. I did rush in headlong. I do it too much, and sometimes it really backfires. I am not playing anyone, but you do see the power of a genuine apology and the willingness to be vulnerable."

"Wow, yeah."

"What do you think might happen if you gave Amanda an apology like that?"

Donny thought for a minute, "I guess if I genuinely apologized for the things I've done wrong, she would probably go into shock."

They both laughed.

"And I don't know that I am ready to hear every-thing she thinks I've done that deserves an apology," Donny added.

"Woo, you hit on a doozy there," Scott said. "Listen, in his book, Relational Leadership, Ford Taylor, lays out the "6-Step Apology" I just gave you, but I've heard him say in public, 'Don't do step 6 with your wife, until you are ready to really listen, and respond with love.'"

"Wow. No kidding." Donny shook his head. "What are the 6 steps again?"

"Step 1: State the offense and be specific. Most conflict requires two people, but you have to take responsibil-ity for your own part. You must let go of what the other person has done. Then there must be NO QUALIFIERS. Qualifiers make the apology about you, not the other person. If you are going to be selfish, don't bother.

Step 2: Say, "I was wrong". No flattery or extra words.

Step 3: Say, "I am sorry." Some say, this is a sign of weakness, but choosing vulnerability has always proven to be a strength for me.

Step 4: Ask for forgiveness. This is where things get tricky, because again, our language can make this about us, and not healing. So, this has to be a request, "Will you forgive me?" Then accept whatever answer the other person gives. If they are not ready to forgive you, you can respond, "Then when you can, I am asking that you will forgive me."

Step 5: Ask for accountability. Give permission for the other person to keep you accountable, but don't require it of them, or this all became about you again. Say, "I give you permission to hold me accountable . . ."

Step 6: Ask if there is anything else. Be ready to receive and apologize for other offenses. If you are going to do this with Amanda, please, do it when you have time to really listen, and hear her heart. Write each offense down, and work through them, giving a 6-Step Apology for each one. (Taylor 2017)

That's the plan." Scott had been writing each step on a napkin as he shared them with Donny. He handed the napkin to Donny.

Donny looked over the napkin. "This won't be easy," he said.

"No," Scott stated matter-of-factly, "but it is often the first step in creating, building, and sustaining great relationships. Choosing vulnerability puts you in a position to bring peace in conflict."

TRAPPED

As Donny drove to work, he reviewed the 6 steps in his head. He thought about how much he needed to apologize to Amanda for and cried.

Arriving at the office a few minutes early, he took a minute to collect himself and text Amanda that he loved her. It was a small step, but it was a step.

As he walked through security, Donny started to notice everything and everyone. He was asking himself if he had reasons to apologize to others with whom he'd had conflict. Then he thought about John. He'd always butted heads with John until this past week, then after listening just a bit to John's story he started to hear John differently.

When Donny got on the elevator and turned around to face the front, he saw John get on.

"Hey, John," he greeted.

"Donny," John acknowledged, then said nothing.

"Hey, John, do you have lunch plans?" Donny asked and almost immediately wondered what he was doing.

"I usually eat in my office and work," John answered. "Want to grab a bite together?"

"No thanks, Donny," John said, "maybe another day."

"Ok," Donny accepted John's answer, but couldn't understand. He had offered an olive branch. What was John's deal? He did always seem to spend lunch in his office. It was like he didn't want any friends.

By the time Donny was heading into the office, he had become almost angry at John for rejecting his offer. He set his brief case down, and was startled by a voice behind him, "Want to grab lunch today?"

Ray and Donny had been friends for years, in fact Ray had helped Donny secure his position as the director of marketing for Munson Logistics, a local transportation company.

"You startled me," Donny admitted.

"Sorry," Ray said.

Immediately Donny thought, Ray should go through all 6-steps. "I'm in," Donny answered. "Where are we headed?"

"How about burgers? I've been wanting to try that new place over on 5th."

"Sounds good." Donny realized in that moment as if by divine inspiration that Ray had worked with John before Donny arrived, so he asked, "Hey, what's up with John Cauley?"

"What do you mean?" Ray asked.

"I don't know, we always seem to butt heads, then Monday I felt like we connected, but when I asked him to lunch, it was like he shut me out again."

Ray stepped into the office and shut the door. Donny felt uncomfortable. Donny didn't like gossip, and Ray could be good at it at times. Donny just wanted to understand.

With the door secure, Ray stepped in and sat at one of the chairs in front of Donny's desk, so Donny sat as well.

"Did you know John's wife left him last year?" Donny had a vague recollection of that happening. "And she left him with the three kids."

"Really," Donny was surprised. Not that someone would leave John, but he had no idea about the kids.

"Ever since, he has been unapproachable. He snaps at everyone. He hides in his little office and counts his beans. He's as frugal as Ebenezer Scrooge, and probably related."

"Woah," Donny stepped in, "Let's not get into name calling. Do you know if he has any friends?"

"Why? Are you thinking about trying to be one?"

"Maybe, if he'll let me."

"Listen," Ray leaned forward in his chair with his elbows propping him up, "John and I used to be friends. We did lunch two to three times a week with our department. Then this happened, and he disappeared. Lunch alone, never time for us after hours. He's as prickly as a cactus. If I were you, I would just let him be."

Just then there was a knock on the door.

"Come in," Donny called.

Sharon, Donny's assistant stuck her head in. "Hey Ray," she greeted pleasantly. Then, "Sorry to interrupt, Donny, but you have the Road Max team coming in 20 minutes, did you need to review anything?"

Donny and Sharon had worked out this cue long ago. Anytime an unscheduled conversation was taking place in his office, she was to give it 3 minutes and interrupt with a need, if Donny told her to "push it", she knew what he was doing was important, if he said, "Let's do it in 5." It meant "Thank you for the save."

While this was important to Donny, the interruption helped him realize that he had the information he needed and should probably get back to work.

"Let's do it in 5," he answered. Then turning back to Ray, he stood up offered his hand and said, "Thanks for the information, and I'll take your input under advisement."

Ray shook his hand with a smile, "Anytime, buddy."

After Ray left, Donny pondered all that he had just learned about his "enemy". He thought about the words of Jesus, "Love your enemies, and pray for them." He decided to start right away.

"Jesus, I have judged John too harshly. I should have been more aware of what was happening. I am sorry. I was wrong. Jesus, please forgive me, and help me to be loving to those who seem to be my enemy. Help me to take the time to understand their needs, and if there is anything else I need to know about John's situation, please, show me. Amen."

The day passed quickly, and Donny headed home. When he came in, he found the place was empty. He quickly called Amanda to make sure everything was ok.

"Hello," Amanda sounded exasperated.

"Hey Babe, I was just checking in. I'm home and didn't know where you were." Donny did his best to sound upbeat and encouraging.

"The girls had talent show tryouts after school today, then we went shopping, and we are just getting done. I'm sorry dinner isn't ready, but I just can't seem to get it all done." Amanda spoke in short bursts with sarcasm dripping from her "apology."

Donny took a deep breath and said, "Ok, can I help with dinner."

"I'm not even sure what I'm doing," Amanda softened slightly.

"Why don't I order pizza tonight?"

"I thought we were trying to save money!" Amanda snapped again.

"I know, but right now it sounds like you getting a breath is more important than savings. Do you want the usual?"

"Fine. I'll talk to you in a bit." Amanda hung up.

As Donny headed to the Wood Street Pizza for one medium cheese and one pepperoni and mushroom pizza, he mulled over his conversation with Amanda. He tried to pray but found himself getting more and more angry. Once again, he hadn't done anything and had his head bit off. Every time Amanda was stressed, Donny felt like he had to walk on eggshells and it was getting old.

More than once he had tried to get Amanda to slow down, but she kept saying, "Yes." Usually to the girls. She felt some need Donny didn't understand to let the girls do everything at school. She also felt the responsibility to show up for everything. The school was creating as many issues as anything since there was an award ceremony every six weeks and an activity every other day, and guilt available in buckets for kids and parents who didn't participate.

Church wasn't any better. They had Sunday morning activities, Wednesday night activities, life groups for the parents, and once a month breakfast for men. It seemed like everywhere Donny turned someone was taking pieces of his family, and they could barely keep up.

By the time he turned back on to his street Donny felt ready to explode, and he hadn't even begun to deal with Amanda. He tried to tell her they had to prioritize, but she just couldn't seem to figure it out. "The only reason I am buying pizza, and we aren't sitting down for a peaceful evening is because she refuses to stop saying, 'yes'." Donny said all this out loud to his windshield, then took a breath.

He pulled into the driveway and breathed. Anger wasn't going to help anyone right now, and he didn't want to fight. Between the car and the door, Donny began to feel better, and the night passed without further incident.

On Sunday, as the family got ready for church, the fireworks started again. This time Katie struggled to get going, Laynie wanted a special hair-do, and Amanda seemed in no hurry to get anywhere. Donny hated being late. His frustration was apparently visible, because Amanda started, "If you're so worried about being late, go ahead without us!"

"Seriously," Donny retorted.

"It's fine," Amanda seemed condescending, "No one will care if we're a little late."

"I'll care!" Donny shouted and stormed out to wait in the car.

Sitting alone, Donny began to feel guilty for losing his temper. What was happening to his family?

After a ride to church, in which the only conversation was figuring out who was taking the girls to class, Donny and Amanda put on the show. They walked into church holding hands, Donny took the girls to class, and they sat together to worship.

When Pastor Frank spoke that morning he shared from James 1:14-15 about the way sin works as it sneaks in and kills. Donny heard some, but really spent most of his time wondering what they were going to eat and how the Hawks would do against the Falcons today.

As they headed to eat after church, Donny noticed Amanda's make-up seemed blotted.

"You ok?" Donny asked.

Amanda rolled her eyes, "Seriously?" She was sarcastic and obviously upset about something, but Donny didn't know what.

Donny didn't want to fight in front of the girls, so he just sat silently.

For the next few days Donny and Amanda shared necessary information and little else. When Tuesday night rolled around, Donny hoped he would get the chance to punch stuff at karate. He was not disappointed.

"Tonight, we will be focusing on our kicks," Scott said after prayer and bowing in. "Every kick has 4 steps. What is the first step to every kick?" Scott pointed to Will, one of the other Dad's Donny had met last week.

"Knee up," Will responded.

That night Donny and the girls learned the proper way to throw a front snap kick. This meant they spent almost 20 minutes kicking the large punching bags all over the dojo. Donny didn't pretend to be kicking anyone in particular, but he did kick with all his pent-up energy. By the time class was finished, he was ready to go to bed.

At the end of class everyone put on sparring gear, which felt awkward, and they were placed in lines facing each other. Each had an opponent about his or her size. Scott gave instructions, "For a few minutes, we are going to practice targeting. Get into your fighting position facing your opponent. Let's start with our right leg back. In this class, we target the front of the body below the neck and above the belt. The sides are legal, but the back, head, and legs are off limits. Now hear me. The reason we avoid striking these areas, is because we don't want anyone injured. So, if you are in real danger, where should you strike?"

"Head, back and legs?" someone answered a bit unsure.

"Yes!" Scott was emphatic. "We only use as much force as is necessary to bring peace, but if someone needs taken down or out, because they are a danger to everyone, you strike where it will do the most damage."

At the end of class as everyone sat listening, Scott started, "Were you surprised by my emphasis on striking where it hurts?" Stunned students sat quietly. "Whenever we talk about defending ourselves from other people, we try to teach you controlled power. So, it is not often I tell you to ignore restraints, but there are two circumstances, in which the restraints are loosened dramatically.

First, if you find yourself defending a crowd from an out of control individual. We have seen too many school shootings lately. If they have a gun, and you can take them down with a strike to the knee, head, or kidney, DO NOT HESITATE! Proper restraint at that point is whatever it takes.

Second, if your enemy isn't human. Too often we forget, 'Our struggle is not against flesh and bone, but against powers and principalities of this dark world.' When you face spiritual enemies, you need to be ready to not hold back. Too often we are too busy being nice to call out sin. This is not loving. The loving thing to do is to attack the enemy with all you have and defend the person caught in the trap.

Jesus says, 'If your brother sins against you, go to him and settle the matter. If he listens, you have won your brother.'

Sin is a trap and as we follow Jesus, as leaders and warriors in his kingdom, we must free whomever, however from sin."

On Thursday, Donny barely pulled himself out of bed in time to get to breakfast with Scott. He considered canceling. He hadn't felt much like growing for the last week and didn't think there would be much to talk about today.

When he got to the diner, Scott all but bounced in and Donny knew he was not in the mood. They ordered from Sarah and talked for a few minutes about the Hawks victory.

Then Scott started, "So how are things at work?"

"Fine," Donny was not in the mood to share feelings today.

"Did you connect anymore with your friend? What was his name? John?"

"John's not really a friend," Donny admitted. "Just a guy I thought I had a connected with."

"Ok. So anymore connection?"

"No, he shut me out again," Donny resisted sharing too much.

"I'm sorry," Scott seemed genuinely concerned.

The food came, and Donny started eating so he wouldn't have to share too much.

"Donny," Scott had his soft voice going. "Have I done something to offend you?"

Suddenly realizing his own desire to be closed was closing off someone who he wanted to trust, Donny's heart softened, "No, I'm just tired. Sorry."

"The trap is set," Scott smiled.

"What trap?" Donny asked.

"The trap of brokenness. I heard a marriage teacher share it once, but I think he got it from somewhere else. The way I like to explain it is that we get TRAPPED. It starts with being tired." Without skipping a beat, Scott grabbed another napkin and pen and dove in.

"You see, every relationship we are in is on a journey. Pastor Frank talked about the last part on Sunday, but it starts before that. We are either growing closer to Jesus or away from Him. The more intimate our relationships are with others the greater the effect on our relationship with God. It also works the other way, the more intimate our relationship is with Jesus, the more intimate we become with others. You with me?"

Taking it all in Donny answered, "Sure."

"Take Amanda for example," Scott wrote her name down, then Donny's, and drew a line between them. He then wrote God above them. "As you and Amanda grow closer to God, you grow closer to each other. He drew two lines connecting Amanda and Donny both to God and creating a triangle." (see Appendix)

The problem is most of us slip into the Trap of Brokenness without realizing it.

The journey begins with being tired. You see, God calls all of us to periods of activity and rest, but as you just said, and as is so true in America, we don't rest. We have abandoned God's plan for Sabbath, because most people think Jesus abandoned it, but he didn't. He just called us to a true understanding of it.

Jesus showed us that the Sabbath is not just about not doing things, it is about being like God. One day a week, God calls us to stop working and give a day to focus on being with Him and like Him. On this one day we should rest or be still from our labor.

Do you know what the Psalms say happens when we are still?" Scott paused to see if Donny was still with him. "The book of Psalms says, 'Be still and know that I am God.' (Psalm 46:10) This is so important. When we don't slow down and get the rest God intends for us it creates a distance. Maybe not a huge distance, but a distance."

"Isn't that what Sundays are for?" Donny asked.

"Well let me answer that this way, how restful was your Sunday?"

Donny thought about the fight he had with Amanda. He had not gone to work, but it was not restful.

Scott continued, "The problem is that when we get tired our growth towards intimacy is over taken by the trap of brokenness."

Scott looked up again and noticed Donny was focused completely on the napkin, so he started writing the steps.

"So, step 1 is we are tired. Step 2 is we become raw. We find ourselves getting our feelings hurt easily because we are extra sensitive, and we respond by lashing out at others because our defenses are on high alert. Whatever the case, grace grows cold. Usually to those closest to us first. This is why, we can be nice to perfect strangers and treat family like our worst enemy. Our raw spirits are more easily and more often offended by those we are closest to.

This is where the trap is set. Our enemy begins to come after us, the Bible says, "Like a roaming lion."

Step 3: we begin to feel alone. Our raw hearts feel hurt so easily by those closest to us, so we decide they don't love us. In reality, we are the ones creating the distance by our own brokenness.

Then step 4: we pull away. Instead of just feeling alone, we begin to separate ourselves. Sometimes we do this with harsh words, sometimes with quiet, sometimes we physically stop being around others.

We are divided from the herd, and the lion prepares to strike.

Step 5: We find ourselves in private sin. We think we are hiding, but the truth is we are giving ourselves over to our desire instead of God. Many people fall into what is considered "acceptable sin." We become workaholics, or binge watchers of television, etc. Women will sometimes put all their energy into the children. Men chase after activity.

Trying to keep up with whatever has captured our hearts besides Jesus, just makes us more tired, and the devil springs his final trap.

Step 6: We become entrenched in sin. At this point, reason leaves the building. We are convinced that we "deserve happiness," and the only way to get it is through some addiction or sin that will only harm us.

This is why people "fall" into adultery. As James says, "We are enticed away by our own desires." We decide to pursue fulfillment through something besides godly intimacy and we find ourselves in the snare of sin. We are no longer in control.

Which leads to step 7: death. Sometimes this is only death of a marriage or friendship, but something always dies, when we get this far."

Scott looked up from the napkin at Donny and noticed tears in his eyes. He said nothing.

Donny stared at the napkin the same way he had stared at his eggs the first time Scott and Donny had breakfast. Finally, he said, "Do you think Amanda could be cheating on me?"

Quietly Scott answered, "I don't know, Donny, but remember sin can come in many forms. This is not just about adultery, it is about giving our heart to anything to bring fulfillment in ways it shouldn't. You should start by asking, if you have cheated on Amanda."

Donny looked up shocked. He saw no judgement in Scott's eyes, no condemnation, but the question stung.

"What do I do?" Donny all but pleaded.

"Apologize. Six-steps." Scott was clear, but not unkind.

"What if she is cheating?"

"Donny, that's a long road, and we're not there yet, but Jesus is alive, so anything can heal.

You have to start with you." Scott set down his pen, as Sarah came back to fill the coffee.

Donny did his best to keep his eyes hidden. When Sarah left, he looked back to Scott and asked, "Pray for me?"

Quickly, Scott responded bowing his head, "Father, Donny has come to a crisis moment. We aren't sure, but it is even possibly a moment of crisis for his marriage. Lord, he needs you to give him courage to face his own brokenness and strength to take ownership of his sin and make amends.

Lord, we pray for Amanda. She too needs your protection and grace.

Jesus you have raised from the dead, and so we know that you can redeem any situation, but we must seek your will and direction. God bring your power to work on Donny and Amanda's marriage. Amen.

Listen," Scott continued, "We may be heading into things, that you and I alone can't handle, but maybe you and Amanda can go to dinner with Kathy and I. We can ask Alex to watch the girls. Can you see if Amanda will go?"

"Sure," Donny was quiet, "and, Scott, thank you."

"You're welcome, Donny, but don't miss this, I just told you what you needed to know. The Holy Spirit moved your heart."

Scott slid out of his seat and paid both bills, while Donny sat and ran everything through his head.

"You gonna be ok today?" Scott asked when he returned.

Donny stood up, "Yeah, I think so. I just have a lot to sort out."

"Good luck," Scott said and gave Donny a hug.

As they left the restaurant, Donny was stunned and sat in his car wondering, "Had he been cheating on Amanda? Was she cheating on him? What would he do if she was? Could his marriage be saved?"

Donny decided to call in to work and take a personal day. He looked at his watch and knew Amanda and the girls would still be getting ready for school, but he called anyway.

"Hey, what's up?" Amanda answered.

"Hey, Honey, have you got plans this morning?" Donny asked.

"I was going to pay bills. Why what's up?" Amanda sounded concerned.

"Well, I just finished my breakfast with Scott and I really think we need to talk. I have something I need to take care of before I come home, but can you meet me after you drop off the girls at school."

"Ok," Amanda still had questions in her voice, "What's going on?"

"God is using Scott to show me some things, and I just need to talk."

"Ok, I guess I'll see you when you get here." Now Amanda sounded exasperated again.

"Amanda, I love you."

"Love you, too." Amanda responded, but it sounded more a force of habit than a confirmation.

Donny went to the local park and prayed, trying to take Scott's advice and start with himself. Suddenly, it all came out, his addiction to his X-box. The way he would watch sports and tune out for hours at a time. Then his heart broke as he began to think about the times he had let ads on his phone lead him to places he knew were wrong.

His mind began to blame Amanda for being so distant. She had pulled away months ago. He couldn't figure out what had happened, but he wondered if she might be in some relationship he didn't know about. As his anger began to rise, Donny realized he was doing what he always did. Blaming someone else for his issues.

By the time he pulled into the driveway, Donny was nervous, but not angry. He still wasn't sure how this conversation would go, but he wanted to find life for his marriage again.

"God, help me," he prayed, and went inside.

Amanda was sitting on the couch when he came in, already paying bills.

"What's wrong?" she asked, and Donny couldn't tell if it was fear or anger in her voice.

"So, remember Pastor Frank's message about sin?"

"Yes," Amanda responded with eyes wide and pulled her knees up to her chest.

"Talking with Scott this morning, I realized there is more to the trap of sin, and I don't want to wait to start changing it.

Amanda, I have not been fair to you. I have allowed myself to be dragged into video games, sports, or whatever else I could to just keep my distance, so we wouldn't fight.

I am sorry.

I was wrong.

Will you forgive me, or when you're ready will you forgive me?

Also, I want you to know that you have my permission to hold me accountable for my time. If you see me pulling away, you can tell me, I am being distant. I love you and want to love you better."

Donny thought about step-six and hesitated.

In the gap, Amanda jumped in, "Is that it?"

Immediately, Donny felt the heat rise to his face. He was trying to apologize, and she wouldn't even let him finish. He was sure she was already gone.

He wanted to make sure he had done his part to do everything right, so he responded with a sarcastic, "You tell me, is there anything else?"

Amanda sat quiet for a minute, then very quietly said, "What about the videos you've been watching?"

Donny was stunned. His defensiveness drained out with the blood from his face.

"I have also been using pornography to sooth myself. It hasn't helped, but I know it is wrong.

I am sorry."

"Why?" Amanda asked.

"Why am I sorry, or why did I do it?"

"Both."

"I am sorry, because it's wrong, and today, Scott helped me see that I was being trapped by sin. I am also sorry I hurt you."

"Do you just need someone prettier? Why would you watch that stuff?"

"I don't know," Donny felt himself getting defensive again. This was not going the way he expected. "It makes me feel wanted! I know it doesn't make sense, but that's the truth. You don't want me, and they make me feel like they do."

"It's not real."

"I know, but real hurts right now!" Suddenly, Scott's words about the trap made sense. Donny pulled the napkin out of his pocket.

"That's the whole problem," Donny softened. "Scott was showing me the trap of brokenness and he showed me that when we start feeling hurt, we pull away into private sin. Then we get entrenched in sin, until something dies.

Private sins can be hidden but obvious sins like pornography, or they can be anything that captures our heart in a way it shouldn't." Donny's eyes were filled with tears as he spoke.

"I am so sorry, Amanda."

Amanda took the napkin and looked at it for a long time.

"I feel alone too, but I don't know what to do about it."

Donny wanted to ask if Amanda was having an affair, but he couldn't bring himself to ask. He noticed she was more and more distant all the time but didn't know when or with whom she could be cheating.

"Scott offered for us to go to dinner with himself and Kathy tomorrow night. Alex could watch the girls, and I think we need the help."

"Ok." Amanda sat quietly staring at the napkin.

After a time, Donny got up and went to work in the garage.

CHOOSE AWARENESS

The rest of the day past and there was peace. It seemed as if someone had let off some pressure from Donny and Amanda's marriage, but in the background, lurked an enemy still waiting to strike.

The next day at work, Donny had a fairly normal day. He spent the morning making calls and setting appointments to meet with clients. He held a brief meeting with one of the associates who reported to him and prepared for the Friday afternoon director's meeting. He was concerned the budget on the upcoming social media growth strategy conference would be a little short. Still his request wasn't outrageous, so he expected approval.

The meeting did not go as planned. John was in rare form, questioning every dollar spent on marketing, and their real value. He and Donny clashed again when Donny tried to explain the future of marketing in social media and John made a joke about playing on Facebook during work hours. John simply did not understand the way the world was shifting.

After the meeting, Donny went back to his office fuming. He had received approval from the vice president, but he was so tired of having to fight John every single time he needed anything. He decided to confront John once and for all.

He knocked on John's office door.

"Open," John said.

"John," Donny started, hoping not to reignite the fight, "We have to figure something out. You and I can't keep fighting every time we're in a meeting together."

John just sat stone faced.

"Have I done something that offended you, that you feel you have to fight me on everything?" Donny asked.

"My job is to make sure this company stays in the black." John said coldly.

"Ok," Donny said, "My job is to make sure we have clients paying us. Why are we not on the same team?"

"We aren't making it."

"What are you talking about?" Donny was shocked. "Our goal for the year was to add 75 new clients, and we've added 82. We should be in good shape."

"We're bleeding somewhere," John said not arguing, but concerned, "and your department goes over budget as much as any."

Donny felt the sting of the last remark.

"Ok, John, how far over are we?" Donny asked, not expecting much.

John turned to his computer and punched a few keys. "Fifteen percent."

"Really," Donny was genuinely stunned.

"Three campaigns have gone over budget. February, April, and May." John turned the monitor, so Donny could see.

Immediately Donny realized all three campaigns were run by the same team, and he had approved the budget. The campaigns were all tremendously creative, but they hadn't brought in enough clients to cover the costs according to the numbers.

"John, how do we know what campaigns bring in what clients?"

"We ask." John sounded surprised that Donny didn't know. "When we send an invoice the clients also receive a survey and we get about 85% of them back. These give us some pretty good stats. How do you not know about this? It's a marketing department issue. Speaking of budgets, the paper for those surveys and ink are costing us too."

"John, I've missed judged you. I am sorry. I did not realize we were over budget so much. I will get with my teams and figure out a plan to be more economical. Is there anything else?"

"Well, honestly, Donny, I need to apologize too. I have a short fuse all the time lately, and you seem to get the brunt of it. The truth is your social media spending is probably the most effective dollar for dollar, but we can't keep breaking the budget."

"I'll make you a deal," Donny said, "What if you and I start meeting weekly, just the two of us, until my department gets this under control?"

"Well, it's not just your department," John was skeptical.

"Maybe not John, but it's a start." Donny offered his hand, "How about Thursdays so we get to the Friday meeting on the same page?"

John looked at his schedule, "I'm not sure when to fit that in."

"How about lunch? You can eat and work in your office like usual, but you'll have company."

John shook Donny's hand, "We'll give it a month and see."

"Great," Donny felt excited, like he had conquered Everest.

"But if we start wasting time, I'm out," John said gruffly.

Donny smiled, "Deal."

As Donny headed home, he thought maybe things were looking up. When he walked in the house, he found the girls sitting quietly on the couch looking like their dog had died.

"Hey girls," Donny walked in and plopped down between them. "What's up?"

"Nothing," Katie said, but it was obviously something.

Donny hugged the girls and went upstairs. He found Amanda putting on make-up. "You ok?" was a dumb question, but he asked it anyway. Amanda just turned and glared.

"What's up with the girls?" Donny asked.

"They have been fighting all day, so I told them to quit, and put them in time out."

"Ok," Donny decided this was a good explanation, and dropped it. "I'm going to change into jeans and meet you downstairs."

When the time came to get in the car and head for Scott and Kathy's the kids were nipping at each other again, and Donny yelled which made Laynie cry. Amanda got upset with Donny for being so harsh, and Donny whipped back that he was doing it for her. All in all, by the time they got to Scott and Kathy's no one was ready to see other people.

The whole family made their way to the strange front door in silence. Over the last few weeks, Donny and the girls had grown a little closer to Scott and Alex, but they had never come to the house. No one was feeling particularly comfortable when Scott opened the door.

"Good evening," Scott said. "Come in to our humble abode."

The ladies filed in and Donny shook Scott's hand and offered a greeting of some sort. Then Alex came around the corner, she put a smile on and greeted the girls warmly. Amanda talked to her for a minute about logistics and tried to give Alex money for pizza.

"We've got that all covered," Scott said. "Come on in and have a seat. Kathy is almost ready."

They sat in the living room on a big couch and the girls headed to the family room on the other side of the kitchen. Abigail and Jordan came downstairs in formation. Jordan was a year older than Katie, and Abigail was a tween, Donny wasn't sure exactly how old.

"Hey girls," Scott said, "the other girls are in the family room." They both started to turn to join in whatever was happening when Scott said a little stern, "Say 'Hello,' to Mr. and Mrs. East."

"Hi," the girls said with little enthusiasm, and went into the family room.

"Sorry," Scott said, "They are usually more friendly."

"It's ok," Donny answered, but he wondered if Scott might have the same issues he did with a house full of girls, emotions and sometimes drama.

"So, Amanda," Scott started, "I've had the chance to get to know Donny better, tell me about you. Are you from here in Springtown?"

"No, I grew up in a small town outside of Des Moines, Iowa called Ames."

"Wow," Scott's interest piqued, "How did you two meet?"

"A friend introduced us in college," Amanda said, "I had grown up with the same on again off again boy, and when I went out of state to Kansas, my roommate wanted to help me move on so she set me up with her best friend's brother."

"Love at first sight?" Scott probed.

"For me," Amanda said, giving Donny a funny look.

Feeling the pressure, Donny jumped in, "I wasn't ready for a commitment with anyone."

"Really?" Scott questioned, "From what I've observed, you seem to be all in on everything."

"Yeah, well 'all in' on marriage was a little scary," Donny started to feel defensive.

"He just wanted to keep his options open," Amanda jibed.

Just then, Kathy came down the stairs. A beautiful lady in every respect, Kathy carried dignity lightly and flowed with a gracious tone all the time. Donny had always thought Scott out did himself.

"Sorry, I'm late," Kathy said. "We had some things not go as planned." She gave Scott a knowing look.

"No worries," Amanda answered as she got up to give Kathy a hug.

"You boys ready," Kathy asked playfully.

"Let's do it." Scott said, and everyone headed for the door.

Kathy turned to the family room and said, "You girls need anything."

"I think we're good," Alex looked up to answer, but went straight back to the game she was playing with the others.

Conversation to the restaurant was pleasant and continued as they waited for a table. Once they were seated and had ordered, Scott turned to Amanda, "Amanda, tell me more about your family."

"Well I have an older brother in Kansas City, and my parents still live in Ames."

"What does your brother do?"

"He's in sales," Amanda answered.

This was Amanda's standard response, the truth was her brother was a pharmaceutical rep for the largest company in the Kansas City area, and had always been a skirt chasing, ladder climbing bachelor who mimicked something out of the television show Madmen. Donny thought Scott should know all this, but he chose to respect Amanda's silence.

"And, I'm sorry, I don't know," Scott continued, "but do you work outside the house?"

"Mostly, I manage some property we own, but otherwise I am with the girls most of the time."

"We really want the girls to have one of us home as often as possible." Donny chimed in.

"That is so good for everyone," Kathy added.

"So, did your mom work?" Scott inquired.

"No, we had a pretty traditional home," Amanda responded almost apologetic.

"Can I push a little? How did you feel about that?" Scott asked.

Amanda looked at Donny. Donny had told Amanda about Scott's propensity to push and his ability to dig out unexpected things. It was clear she was skeptical.

"Honey, maybe not now," Kathy jumped in.

Scott looked at her, then back at Amanda, "I'm sorry, Amanda. I tend to always be in coach mode."

"It's ok," Amanda relaxed. "I have really never thought about it. Mom was just always at home, but it always just seemed to me that my mom lacked ambition."

"Have you ever asked her about it?" Kathy asked.

"No," Amanda was clearly uncomfortable under these questions, but Donny knew this might help her, help them. So, he stayed quiet.

"I'm sorry, Amanda," Scott said, "We don't want to make you uncomfortable. We have just learned that knowing someone's past can really make an impact on how you love them."

Kathy and Scott smiled at each other, then Kathy asked, "Can I tell them?" Scott smiled and raised his hand palm up indicating she should go ahead.

"About ten years ago, Scott and I had reached rock bottom. The girls were young, we were running all the time, and Scott was so busy we barely met each other for a few minutes at the end of each day. We both found ourselves growing apart. That's when we learned about the TRAPPED model, Scott shares. Have you seen it?"

Donny and Amanda both nodded.

"Well we also learned about the Seven Daily Choices of Relationships. The first is vulnerability. We must be willing to open ourselves up to each other, and not only recognize our weaknesses, but admit to them. There is a six-step apology model we learned for sharing mistakes. We also learned the need to choose awareness. This was a big choice for me. I didn't realize how often I was hurting Scott, because I had never asked a lot of important questions...of him or of me.

The more I began to understand Scott the easier it was for me to show him love in ways that really helped his heart to feel safe. That's the next choice, but I don't want to get ahead of myself. What amazed me was how much I didn't know, because I had never tried to know. I was so self-focused, thinking I understood how everybody thought or should think."

She looked at Scott, "Poor Scott. His heart was shriveling up, not because this wonderful breath of fresh air wasn't in him, but because I didn't know how to help him flourish. The more I began to learn about him, the more I changed the way I showed him love.

The more I changed, the more he changed. Now we are as happy as we have ever been. I think?" She turned to Scott playfully looking for assurance.

"Almost heaven," Scott assured her with enthusiasm. Then he started turning his head every which way as if searching for lost treasure.

"What are you doing, Honey?" Kathy asked.

"Cloth napkins. I am looking for something to write on."

Kathy and Donny both laughed. Amanda turned to her purse and pulled something out. "Maybe use the back of this," she suggested, as she handed Scott the napkin with the TRAPPED framework on one side. Donny had no idea she was carrying it around.

"I see you know Scott's work." Kathy jibed. Scott smiled at her. Amanda never smiled, she just waited.

Scott pulled the pen from his shirt pocket and dove in, "When we are choosing awareness, we have to mind our ps and qs." Donny and Amanda glanced at each other wondering what Scott meant. "You see," Scott continued, "that phrase is used to suggest we be on our best behavior, but one possible etymology of the phrase, has to do with bartenders keeping an eye on how many "pints and quarts" a patron had so as not to send him home too drunk, or for the patron to be aware of how much he has had. Either way, the idea was that you needed to be aware of the circumstance and behave accordingly.

In relationships, we "mind our ps and qs" by understanding what we need to know about a person to treat them fairly, and how we learn it." Scott glanced up to make sure he hadn't lost anyone.

"Our "ps" are the four understandings we need to gain to treat people well:

1. Past hurt.

   We have a tendency to hurt people unknowingly sometimes, because we don't know enough about how they were raised or taught. There is a whole teaching on the hippocampus, but let's stay focused.

2. Present struggles.

   Sometimes we treat people unfairly, because we don't understand their circumstance. Stephen Covey says, "Seek first to understand, then to be understood." In his book, 7 Habits of Highly Effective People, Covey tells the story of a time he misjudged a man for letting his kids run wild on a subway train. Until the man told him they had just come from the hospital, where his wife, their mom, had died, and he wasn't sure how to behave either. Circumstances change the way we perceive other people's choices, but when we are unaware of their present struggles, we make bad assumptions." (Covey 1989)

Donny thought about John, and how he had misjudged him. Awareness might be the key to changing their relationship.

Scott continued, "Can you see how these things might change a relationship?

3. Personality.

   We all have different personalities that effect the way we see and interact with the world. Maybe you have heard of the DiSC profile. You can actually find a bunch of good systems for helping you understand yourself and each other, but there is a free assessment for DiSC at www.123test. com/disc-personality-test. Understanding this basic assessment allowed us," Scott indicated himself and Kathy, "to really understand why we did some of the things we do, and why.

4. Private Love Language.

    Each of us has our own way of giving and receiving love. While there are five general languages identified by Gary Chapman in his book, The 5 Love Languages, each combination and dialect is unique to an individual. A lifetime of adventure lies in discovering the depths of someone else's personal love language. You can get a basic assessment at www.5lovelanguages.com. (Chapman 2000)

Still with me?" Scott glanced up to see Donny and Amanda leaning forward to see the napkin clearly.

"The problem we all find, is that even when we understand what we need to be aware of, we still don't know how to become aware. So, we need to mind our 'qs':

1. Quick to listen.

    Sometimes we are moving so fast through life, we miss what really matters. Too often we equate listening with hearing, but listening is about learning. When we listen, we are trying to gain new knowledge or insight. That means we don't just listen with our ears to what people are saying. We listen with our eyes to how they are acting. We listen with our mind to their tone of voice and stature. Finally, we listen with our heart to changes in emotions. We all see these aspects of life every day, but the wise person seeks to understand these responses in order to understand how to care for people better.

2. Question first.

When we are trying to build and empower thriving relationships, we need to learn to ask more questions than we answer. I recognize the irony that I am talking a lot; however, if you remember this conversation started with us trying to get to know each other better."

Scott looked Amanda in the eye, "We will get back to that.

We also need to be sure to use "Learner" questions versus "Judger" questions. Marilee Adams, in her book, Change Your Questions/Change Your Life, does a fantastic job of explaining the difference that takes place when we are trying to understand others instead of instruct or convince them. (Adams 2004)

3. Quiet your answers.

When we do respond or teach, we need to be sure our whole heart is for the other person in the relationship. Too often, we rush in with answers when we should still be asking questions, or when we give answers, they are the ones we want to give, not the ones people are asking.

There is a time to give answers, but they must be thoughtful and kind, trying to benefit the other person. We must consider past hurt, present struggle, personality, and private love language, as well as timing and intent. Giving a productive answer is hard, so we should be slow to give any."

Scott sat back and looked at the napkin to make sure he hadn't missed anything, then looked at Donny and Amanda. Dinner had arrived, and Scott hadn't eaten much, but started in now. The others were mostly done.

The silence weighed as a stark contrast to Scott teaching. Then Donny shared the story of what had happened with John earlier that day at work, and how awareness made the difference. The rest of dinner past with normal conversation, as the two couples spent time getting to know each other better.

On the way home, Amanda was quiet as the girls chittered away about all the things they had done. Donny took time to help the girls get in bed then came back downstairs to Amanda sitting on the couch drinking a cup of tea. He went to the kitchen grabbed a glass of water and joined her.

"Scott's pretty intense, isn't he?" Donny asked.

"That's an understatement," Amanda quipped. They both sat silent as they thought through the night.

When it grew uncomfortable Donny said, "That's pretty much what breakfast is like every Thursday. Did you have a good time getting to know Kathy?"

"I know Kathy," Amanda sounded offended and shocked that Donny seemed so oblivious.

"What did I do?" Donny felt his own spirit getting offended by her short answers.

Amanda didn't answer quickly. When she did, she looked Donny straight in the eye, "How come you can slow down to understand some guy at work, but you never have time to try understanding me?"

The question stung, especially after all Scott had taught them tonight. Donny knew he should just stay quiet, but his tongue took over, "Maybe if I didn't get my head bit off every time I asked a question, I would ask more." Donny got up and stormed into the garage to work on a project.

He really couldn't find anything to do, so he spent his time, straightening his tools while he tried to calm down. "Why can't we have a serious conversation for longer than two minutes without fighting?" He wondered. "What was it that caused his anger to flare up so quickly? Why did Amanda not seem to care about anything he said?" Donny looked down at the wrench in his hand and felt it press into his fist as he squeezed as tight as he was able. He was tempted to throw the wrench against the wall, but common sense took back over, so he just put the wrench in the tool box forcefully. "Besides," he thought to himself, "if you put a hole in the wall, you have to fix it, Stupid."

When Donny final went up to bed, the lights were off, and Amanda was quiet. As he lay down staring at the ceiling, he finally started to drift off, and heard crying.

BUILD

CHOOSE SAFETY

The next few days were filled with tension. Donny could feel himself ready to blow up at almost anything and did in short bursts. After a few nights sleep, the reality of living together had kicked back in and the tension withdrew a bit but didn't go away.

When Tuesday night rolled around, Donny didn't have opportunity to talk to Scott before class. The routine was normal for the first 30 minutes or so, the class spent time on basic skills and then time learning kata. Then Scott called the class back together early, "Today we are going to take a few minutes to learn some Aikijitsu." Donny had heard of it. He really didn't know the difference from one martial art to the other but was interested to learn something different.

"At this point we have all learned our parry block and are learning our angles. The two most used angles are angle one and three," he pointed to a giant chart on the wall with an eight-pointed star and the numbers 1-11 in seemingly random order. "There are eight angles of evasion and balance, and another three added for attacks, but we will learn about attacking in the advanced class. Self-defense starts with being in what we call the 'good spot.'" With a wave us his hand Scott asked Jeff to come help him demonstrate, "The 'good spot' is on the back side between the shoulder and elbow. My goal in any defensive situation is to get here," Scott pointed again between Jeff's shoulder and elbow.

"Whether someone attacks you with a fist, a weapon, or tries to grab you, your objective is to get here." Scott took a minute to instruct Jeff on what he wanted Jeff to do. Then Jeff attacked, and with a parry block and one step, Scott was in what he had called "the good spot." Scott's speed impressed Donny.

"From here," Scott continued as Jeff stayed in position, "I can do whatever comes naturally." Scott proceeded to simulate multiple ways to abuse Jeff, and the class laughed.

Next, Scott had the class partner up with someone about their own size and practice moving to "the good spot." After a few minutes, he called the class back together and had them sit for his teaching.

"The goal is to get to the good spot. In a broader sense, this one concept can keep you safe most of the time. Who knows how many times I have used my physical martial arts skill to protect myself from an attacker?"

Several students said, "Never." Donny had never thought about it. Scott had been training in the martial arts for over 20 years and had never needed to use his training to defend himself. Then Donny thought about his own life and realized he wasn't sure when or where he would use this training.

Scott said, "Self-defense begins when we choose to be in good spots. Simply, don't do stupid. There are four 'stupids' we need to avoid. Don't be in stupid places, at stupid times, doing stupid things, with stupid people. Now I know we shouldn't call people stupid, but when you are participating in activities that can harm you for no reason other than you are not thinking first, that is stupid. Self-defense starts when we decide to think about where we are, who we are with, what we are going to do and when.

We've told you before about the ten-year-old who was about to get her black belt and was asked by a panel member, who was a grown man, 'You are barely 5 feet tall, and probably don't weigh 100 pounds wet. If you run into a guy my size in a dark alley, what do you think you are going to do?' to which she replied, 'Why would I ever go in a dark alley?'

Listen, this also applies to our relationships. Leadership is influence, which means it is all about relationship. Safety in relationships also comes down to getting to the 'good spot'. When we have conflict in our relationships, too often we strike back with our tongue or our attitude and treat people we care about poorly. Instead we need to choose safety. Safety comes when we choose first to move to a good spot. The Bible says, 'speak the truth in love.' That last phrase, 'in love', indicates we need to be careful about when, where, how, as well as what we say. The when, where, and how are about keeping us and the person we have conflict with safe. While we need honesty for relationships to flourish, the level of honesty is directly connected to the level of safety. If we do not create a safe environment for people to hear truth, then they won't hear it, even if we say it. We must seek to create safety first."

As Scott finished and started to close class, Donny found himself eager for more. He understood that when, where, and how made a difference in the ability to communicate, but based on he and Amanda's recent conversations, he clearly didn't know how to create this safety. Unfortunately, after class Scott wasn't available, and Donny knew they were meeting for breakfast on Thursday, so he typed his questions into his phone to be sure he asked them then.

When Thursday rolled around, Donny got to the diner early. Scott arrived, and they exchanged pleasantries and ordered their food. By now Sarah knew what both men wanted, and simply checked to be sure.

"So, I want to talk about safety," Donny started in almost desperate to find answers.

"Ok," Scott smiled. "How can I help?"

"You said on Tuesday that safety in relationships comes down to where, when, how, and what we say, but apparently right now, I can't ever get it right with Amanda."

"That bad, huh?" Scott asked.

"Even as I have been trying, nothing is working. I am trying to be vulnerable and think about what Amanda and the girls need. I am struggling with feeling tired, but I think there is more. No matter what I do, Amanda is holding back."

"Well, before we went out this weekend you wondered if she might be having an affair." Scott reminded him.

"Yeah, I am past that, but something is up, because she won't talk to me."

"Ok, well I am going to focus on safety today, because honesty is another conversation. However, you need to know that the level of honesty in a relationship is directly connected to the level of safety felt in that relationship. Maybe if you understand how to help Amanda feel safer, you can help her open up."

"That would be great!" Donny replied.

"So, creating safety comes down to A, E, I, O, and U," Scott grabbed a napkin and took out his pen. "I told you the other day we need to consider when, where, how, and what we say based on five rules:

A – Appreciate Differences

Men and women are different, and no matter, how the world tries to make this simple, there are as many 6500 genetic difference between the sexes. The two key differences you must understand are the differences of brains and needs.

First, our brains are different. When boys are born, testosterone floods their brain and severs many of the connections between the two hemispheres. This allows men to think in boxes. Creating space for each thought and evaluating it based on its own merit. Girls are flooded with estrogen, which does not sever the connections. This allows women to connect the dots. All the dots. Mark Gungor does an incredible job in his video "The Tale of Two Brains" which you can watch on YouTube, explaining this difference:

https://www.youtube.com/watch?v=3XjUFYxSxDk

Second, the core needs of men and women are different. Men, at their core, need honor. They need to feel valued. They need to understand their value and feel that others close to them respect them. Women need to feel secure. In their core, there is a need to have confidence that everything, and everyone is going to be ok. When Kathy and I were getting married, this was the main focus of our pre-marital counseling. Pastor Frank said, 'Every fight you have will come down to Kathy not feeling secure or me not feeling valued or both.' Over time I have discovered that this is not a hard and fast rule for all men and women, but it is a general rule.

I have also found that when we choose generosity and gratitude, we can produce both feelings of value and safety. So, think outside the box. Make a point of saying 'Thank you.' Go above and beyond what is necessary on a daily basis, and you will begin to shift the mood of your home.

E – Encourage Strengths

God has created each of us uniquely. Far too often we ridicule our uniqueness instead of honoring it. But when we honor one another's strengths we create a home, workplace, church, community that doesn't expect the impossible of people, and still encourages greatness. Too many times, I see safety die the death of a thousand cuts, as couples or friends jibe at each other, little by little destroying trust and intimacy.

Instead, we should try building one another up one brick at a time. Discover the unique traits that we each possess and honor them. Every time we offer a moment of approval for someone else's gifts, we create a safer environment, if we are being honest in our appraisal.

I – "I" Language

Especially in conflict, we need to use I language with a giving focus. 'I have a problem.' 'I need help'

'I am hurt.' We need to understand that the way we
see the world and current circumstance is limited to
our point of view. We cannot spend our time blaming others but taking responsibility for our issues.

O – Open Your Stance

This is a martial arts metaphor. Instead of facing off
eye to eye with our "opponent", we should choose to
stand shoulder to shoulder, ready to surrender our
position for the sake of the relationship. So often
we fight for the position we think is right, instead of
choosing to be right. I mentioned Tuesday, "Speak
the truth in love." Love is not self-seeking.

When Jesus tells us to love our enemies, the word
means 'those with whom we have strife.' This is
usually someone we do love or at least care about,
so we need to learn to open ourselves up. When
we do, we often find we are trying to accomplish
the same goal. This gives us the ability to work
together against a common problem, instead of
against each other.

U – Unlock Your History

Sometimes safety can be achieved by taking time
to remember why you came together. What is the
goal you share? In marriage we can gain clarity by
remembering why we fell in love. What was it that
caused you to choose Amanda above everyone
else. Remember her as she was and then recognize
what is still there."

Scott sat back and pushed the napkin across the
table.

"I'm getting a collection of these," Donny smiled.

"Sorry, Kathy keeps telling me I need to write this all down, but so far, I like creating on the fly." Scott smiled back.

After light conversation, both men said their good-byes and headed out to get on with their days. Donny struggled to focus at work even in his meeting with John, instead he kept thinking about the framework Scott had shown him. He knew he needed to create a safer environment for Amanda, especially dealing with his temper. He also prayed they could find a way back from their relationship brokenness.

CHOOSE HONESTY

Over the weekend, Donny was intentional about everything he did. Trying to create a safer environment for Amanda and the girls. He wanted desperately to find a way back to Amanda but knew it might take a long time. Still each day he could try.

On Saturday, after mowing the lawn he sat down to watch Mark Gungor's video on YouTube. He was laughing so much the girls all stopped what they were doing and watched with him. Donny looked at them and began to see how they were so different from him. He also began to think about what made each one of them special.

By Tuesday, there was a sense of peace, beginning to take hold. As Donny drove home from work to get the girls for Karate, he thought about how quickly his home had shifted. He wasn't fooling himself into believing everything was fixed, but he could see that everyone was getting along better, and he and Amanda had been physically intimate for the first time in a long time.

After church on Sunday, Scott had suggested that Donny try writing a letter to "the Amanda he married," telling her why he loved her. The exercise had caused Donny to see his bride in Amanda again, even though he hadn't shown it to anyone.

After praying and bowing in, Scott started teaching about offensive versus defensive moves. "Last week we talked about safety being a matter of getting to the good spot, but we also need to know what to do once we are there. Today we will be following up our blocks and shifts with strikes. Whenever someone attacks there is always an opening to influence their next decisions."

For the next 30 minutes Scott lead the class through a series of drills showing them where to target strikes to be the most effective. Each drill built on the one before. By the time the class broke up to work on kata, Donny found himself getting into a rhythm of blocking, sliding and striking that surprised him. After only a few weeks he and the girls began to feel like they belonged here. When Scott gathered the class together again, Donny was feeling good.

"There is always an opening," Scott started. "Whenever we choose to move out of the line of fire, into a good spot, there is always a place of influence we can strike. We train ourselves to begin seeing the opening. So that when openings come we are always prepared.

In relationships, there is also an always. We say it every week. What do we always choose?"

"Honesty," the whole class responded.

"Right. When we choose to be honest always, we leave no doubt for others about us. Our character never needs defended, because we are striving to always be honest. When we speak the truth, we need to do so in love, but we should always speak the truth. Sometimes the truth hurts doesn't it? But as one of my Senseis likes to say, 'Pain is a suggestion of direction.'

If we want to help others to become their best selves, and we want relationships that are thriving and productive, we will *always* lead with honesty."

Scott knelt, and everyone began reciting the Good Fight Creed,

> "I come to you with only karate, my empty hands.
> I am a law-abiding citizen.
> I seek peace.
> I have respect for others and myself
> I take responsibility for all my words and actions.
> I show caring to everyone.
> I am honest ALWAYS.
> This is my creed, karate."

Breakfast started in the usual way on Thursday. Scott and Donny shared life for quite a while before Scott asked, "So, how are things with Amanda?"

"They seem better this week," Donny replied gratefully.

"Good, what do you think is the difference?"

"Well, to be honest," Donny started.

"Always," Scott quipped.

Donny smiled, "Right. I have been really intentional about minding my ps and qs. I also have started spending time with my Bible every morning. Well, my Bible app."

"Youversion?" Scott asked.

"Yeah, they have these great devotionals. They are helping me keep my mind right."

"God is so good to reveal our own hearts more clearly when we spend time with Him and read His word," Scott sounded almost choked up. His eyes even teared up a little.

"You, ok?" Donny asked.

"Yes," Scott smiled. "Sometimes I am overwhelmed by the goodness of the Lord. So, you said you and Amanda are doing better, is there something in particular."

"Well, not necessarily. We just seem to have re-connected."

"Sex?" Scott asked, and Donny was shocked by the forwardness of the question.

"Yeah, actually," Donny felt uncomfortable.

"Listen, sex is hardly the only sign of intimacy, but good sex is all but impossible in a relationship that doesn't have intimacy. Just be careful."

"What do you mean?"

"Well, for you, sex makes you feel connected to your wife. It opens her up to you and you to her, but for her she is giving her whole self because she feels safe. If you are not careful to protect her, it will be harder to recover next time."

"Wow, I never thought about that." Donny sat quiet and asked himself if he had been selfless in intimacy. Had he continued to try being safe after he and Amanda had shared that night. He thought he had but wasn't sure.

Scott broke the silence, "Listen, Donny, in any relationship, when someone opens a door to their heart, even a little, we have to show genuine appreciation. We have to give them a reason to believe it mattered.

For most people, just cracking the door is scary, so anytime someone does we need to show them our gratitude."

"Well, believe me I am grateful."

"But have you shown it?"

Donny started to answer, then stopped.

"Unexpressed gratitude feels like ingratitude, and ingratitude repels the heart." Scott said. (Stanley 2018)

Donny let those words run in his head. "Wow, Scott, that's a deep thought. I am not sure I have expressed my gratitude."

"Tuesday, I talked about being honest, well that starts with getting honest with yourself, by getting honest with God. Then being honest with others gets easier. Your time in the Bible has opened you to the Holy Spirit, and so some of this reflection will happen without you thinking about it too much, but the big take-aways will come when you meditate on the ideas. Sometimes, honesty can sting, but 'pain is a suggestion of direction.'" Scott looked at his watch.

"Are we still getting together tomorrow night?" Scott asked.

"Oh yeah, I forgot, but I think so," Amanda had made these plans with Kathy at church, the Roland's were coming over for a cook-out. Donny realized he needed to go get the meat.

"Well, I have to get going," Scott said, "But tomorrow night, remind me to explain what honesty shows us."

"Ok," Donny agreed.

As Donny paid the bill and headed to work, he thought about unexpressed gratitude, and ordered Amanda flowers.

The next evening Donny left work early to get home and help Amanda get ready for company. As everyone worked hard to get ready, Donny noticed that no one was complaining. He had to push Laynie once or twice, but all in all attitudes remained positive, and the stress level stayed low.

When the Roland's arrived, Donny noticed the same discomfort on the faces of the girls, his family had felt going into their house the first time. Laynie hugged everyone, and it brought the tension down.

"Enter our humble abode," Donny tried to be light hearted, acting like a royal vizier, but he felt dumb afterward. Still, no one seemed to mock. Scott shook Donny's hand as he entered, and the Family went into the living room, where Amanda had set up enough chairs for everyone, but Laynie and Katie, who sat on the floor most of the time.

Once everyone was in, Amanda headed for the kitchen to finish things up. Donny had finished cooking the burgers 5 minutes before their guest arrived, and he decided to entertain until dinner was ready.

"Katie and Laynie," Amanda called from the kitchen, and Katie immediately responded.

"Laynie, your mom called," Donny made sure she heard. He was pretty sure she had but figured being gentle was the best follow up.

"Sorry," Donny said to his guests.

"No problem," Scott said.

The girls came back in to take everyone's order, and Abby, Scott's oldest, got up to help. Soon everyone was sitting at dinner sharing stories.

Donny thoroughly enjoyed getting to know more about Scott's family, and seeing them interact with each other. Scott had always seemed a bit too right, but this time helped Donny and Amanda both to see that this family was more like his than he would have believed. Somehow sharing stories of joys and mistakes made everyone seem bonded by the time the food stopped moving.

When everyone finished, the girls, except Abby went into the living room to watch a movie together.

"Well, that was nice," Kathy said.

"It was, wasn't it," Donny responded, "I felt like we fit together."

"Food will do that," Scott said. "It is amazing how often, putting good stuff in our mouth will open our hearts."

Everyone sat quiet, and Donny contemplated what Scott had said. Suddenly, he began to feel uncomfortable, as the conversation had stopped. So, he started a new one, "Hey Scott, you said I was supposed to remind you to tell me about what honesty does."

"Actually, I asked you to remind me to tell you what honesty shows," and for a moment Scott looked lost. Donny got up and grabbed a Walmart bag. He handed it to Scott. Scott smiled and then pulled out a new package of napkins and pens.

Everyone laughed.

"Now you can write that book Kathy keeps telling you to write," Donny joked, and they all laughed again.

As Scott started unwrapping the napkins, Donny noticed Kathy give Abby a look that suggested she go watch the movie, and she reluctantly left the table.

New napkin and pen in hand, Scott didn't hesitate, "You see, Donny, honesty and safety go hand in hand. When we act on A, E, I, O, and U, we create an atmosphere where we feel safe to share our thoughts, feelings, failures, and joys. As long as we maintain the environment of safety the freedom to be honest grows. But our enemy, will still plague us with fear. He will use our past hurts or someone else's brokenness to cause us to fear being completely open. We withhold some of the truth, because we don't want to get hurt, be hurtful, or lose something precious to us.

The problem is that while we keep something broken in the dark it has more power to do harm than if we bring it into the light. It's like Seymour's flytrap from

Little Shop of Horrors. We feed our brokenness in the darkness on fear, and it grow, but if it stays in darkness it has power. Many times, bringing something into the light brings hurt and struggle, but the fear loses its power. There is no hurt that can't be healed once it is revealed.

So, honesty *shows* us how to be free."

At this point Scott started writing on the napkin:

1. "Honesty shines light in darkness. As I just said, honesty shines light in the darkness of our hearts. It begins the process of healing. When we keep things hidden we create unsafe space, and so the fear and brokenness grow.

2. Hinders self-deception. One of the greatest hang-ups for any relationship is the belief that our sins will remain hidden. Often sin's grip is obvious to everyone around us, but we think we are keeping it hidden. They may not know all the details, but they can sense its grip on you. Of course, the longer we try to hide sin, the bigger it gets, and it will eventually come out. Honesty keeps us from fooling ourselves into thinking 'little' sins will remain little.

3. Opens us up to growth. When we are willing to live with openness before others, we become more what God intended. We are not stuck in one place. Honesty gives us the ability to be teachable and grow. We become better people.

4. Works always. Sometimes we think that we are better off not sharing certain secrets, and while I would say there is wisdom in not sharing every secret with everybody, *someone* should know

or be able to know everything. The truth is you will find more safety when you have two or three people who can know everything.

Sometimes we don't want to hurt people's feelings, so we hold back. While tact, which is more about timing and phrasing, is good. The truth is always best. I recently heard the actor Christ Pratt giving advice to an Mtv audience. One of his points was 'if you have to give a dog medicine, wrap it in hamburger.' Now, I don't know if he meant to be deep, but since much of the rest of his speech was deep, I wonder. Still, the point is, that we need to express the truth in a way that is compassionate, but we must express it none-the-less.

Anytime the truth stays hidden, darkness gains power.

More importantly, the expressed truth alone has the power to begin healing, even as it hurts. Like a surgeon with a scalpel, the truth separates bone and marrow to bring healing to broken places.

When Scott finished, he set the pen down, and everyone sat quiet. Donny noticed Scott give Kathy a concerned look. Whatever passed between them, he could see she was giving him permission to make a decision.

"I need to be honest with you guys about something we found out today." Scott said, and Donny began to worry. "We went to the doctor today, because I haven't been feeling right for several weeks, and I have been diagnosed with stage 2 colon cancer. The doctor says my prognosis is good, but I may have to spend some time in the hospital fighting it. I just want you to know that these last few weeks have been great for me, and I wanted to ask you guys to pray for us. We need as many people around us as possible.

Jeff knows, and if he needs to he will be taking some of my classes. I don't know what will happen with our Thursdays, but we will work it out. Sorry, to kill a great time, but we needed to tell you."

Donny sat stunned, what could be said. Amanda started to cry quietly, she was trying not to bother the girls. She got up and went to the bathroom to gather herself.

"The girls know," Kathy said, "and we are not keeping this a secret. So, you don't need to worry about that."

"Wow," Donny answered. "I am so sorry, Scott." Donny was overwhelmed by Scott's openness, by the gravity, by the reality for him, by how quickly he had come to care for this family, and by the possible loss. Amanda returned.

"Do you guys have any questions?" Scott was being too gracious.

"No," Donny and Amanda answered.

"We're going to be ok," Kathy offered, "but we wanted you to know." Amanda hugged her, and they both cried.

After a few minutes, Scott said to Kathy, "Didn't we bring pie! Enough sadness. If we are going to fight together, we need strength and courage, and nothing gives strength and courage like lemon pie!"

The girls laughed lightly, then got up to cut and distribute pie. Donny still couldn't speak. His problems seemed so small right now. Scott was facing death, literally, and he still encouraged others. Donny wished he could be that strong.

After the pie and more conversation, the evening wound down. As the Roland's headed out the door, and everyone offered their good-byes, hugs were exchanged all around. "I'll be praying," Donny said, as he hugged Scott like a brother.

"Thank you," Scott said. Their eyes met and for a moment Donny knew that his care for Scott was genuine and mutual.

SUSTAIN

CHOOSE FORGIVENESS

After Donny helped the girls to bed, he came back downstairs to find Amanda crying softly on the couch. He sat next her and pulled her into his arms, and she sobbed.

After what seemed like an hour, she pushed away, "I'm so sorry, Donny," she said.

"Me too," Donny replied. "Scott has taught me so much in such a short time. I don't think I have ever experienced anything like it." Amanda just sat staring into her Kleenex. Donny reviewed the night during the silence and remembered the honesty lessons. Honesty clearly could hurt, but would he be happier not knowing? Maybe, but he would not be healthier.

Amanda picked up her phone, opened an app and began searching. Donny wondered why she would do this right now. Amanda started crying again. Then she turned to Donny and said, "I know my timing is horrible, but with everything we talked about tonight, I need you to see this, and know *I am sorry*."

Her last three words were emphatic, and Donny wondered what she could possibly be talking about. He looked at the email thread she had opened. The conversation with Amesman91@gmail.com meant nothing to Donny at first, but only a few sentences in he realized what it was. Amanda had been emailing her high school sweetheart, Braydon. The emails started innocuously, but quickly became intimate. The more he read, the angrier he became.

Amanda waited. Donny read. How could she do this to him? He knew something was going on. As he started looking at the dates, he realized that this thread was 6 months old.

"So, this is why you hate me," Donny seethed. "You want him."

"No, I don't." Amanda cried.

"Really," Donny's voice was rising, he could feel the tension, "These emails would suggest otherwise."

"I know," Amanda admitted, "I don't know what I was thinking. I was hurt. You were angry all the time and distant. It seemed like our whole life was falling apart. Braydon got a hold of me through Facebook, and it just happened."

"This doesn't just happen! You made a choice!" Donny was almost shouting.

"You'll wake the girls," Amanda chided.

"You think I care right now!"

"You never care!" Amanda shot back.

Suddenly, Donny could see it all. The trap, the attack, the enemy had them.

Donny stopped, breathed, sat down, and waited.

In the quiet, he heard Laynie crying. He went upstairs to check on her. His anger was rising again as he went up, but he knew it wasn't Laynie's fault.

When he went into the room, Katie was up too. "We heard you fighting," Katie said.

"Ok," Donny answered. "We will try to stop. Go back to sleep. I will check on you later."

Donny kissed both girls on the forehead and went back downstairs, trying not to let anger get the better of him. He sat back down and thought.

Final he asked, "When you went home last time, did you see him?"

"Yes," Amanda answered softly.

Donny's rage surged, but he tried to restrain it, "And?"

"And what?"

"Did you sleep with him?"

"No!" Amanda seemed offended that Donny had even asked. Donny was ready to explode. "He wanted to, but I said, 'No,'" she admitted.

"Did anything happen?"

"No," this time Amanda was quiet. "I wanted to, but I knew it was wrong."

The admission of desire was too much for Donny to bare. He glared with anger at Amanda. He could feel the heat rising in his hands. Suddenly, images of his father hitting his mother popped in his head. He jumped up from the couch and went outside.

He thought about driving until he went off the road, but had left the keys inside, and wasn't going back in. Instead, he texted Scott, "Are you still up? I need to talk?'

Instead of a text, his phone rang.

"Hey, Scott."

"Hey, what's up?" Scott sounded almost cheerful. How could he do that with all he was going through?

"She didn't cheat exactly, but Amanda has been communicating with her old boyfriend from high school."

"I am sorry, Donny." Silence.

"I knew something was going on. I told you." As Donny began to spill his anger rose again. "They've been emailing back and forth for 6 months. 6 months! Then she saw him when she went home a few months ago, and he tried to sleep with her. Scott I am so mad I just want to punch things!"

"Well don't." Then quiet again.

"What do I do Scott?"

"What do you want to do?"

"I don't know. I am so angry. I have been trying so hard and now this. I know your stuff is life and death, but this feels that way."

"I'm sure it is worse. No one is to blame for my pain."

"Right!" Donny couldn't seem to hold back the anger. He turned to look inside the house for the first time and saw Amanda on her knees crying and looking like she was praying. His heart softened. "I love her, Scott. I do, but this, this betrayal. I don't know."

"Donny, I am going to be pointed. Are you ok with that?"

"Yes."

"A little over a month ago, God put you in my path. Your marriage was falling apart, and you didn't know what to do. Your relationships at work were fractured and frustrating, and you were lost. As we have spent time together, I have seen a man who wants to get life right, a good man, but a man who too often sees the fault in others before himself.

Over the last weeks, you have grown. You have admitted to your flaws and moved away from them. You have changed the way you see the world. I believe the Holy Spirit is revealing himself to you and through you, so right now you have another choice to make, will you keep following his ways, or turn aside?"

Donny felt encouraged and chastised, admonished was the word. He knew everything Scott just said was the truth. He knew God was at work in his life. It didn't remove the hurt, but it brought an unexpected peace. "I want to follow God." Donny was clear.

"Then race to forgive her."

"I'm not sure how."

"Donny, I don't have a napkin, and we shouldn't take time to dive deep right now but listen, you need to race to forgive her. Don't wait another moment. Let's do breakfast in the morning. Ok?"

"Ok."

Donny went back inside, and Amanda looked up from her place on the floor. He wasn't sure what to say. "Race!" Donny heard Scott's voice in his head. He took three strides, knelt to his bride, and gathered her in his arms. They both wept.

"I'm so sorry," Amanda finally said again.

Donny lifted her face in both hands and stared deeply into her eyes. Held her gaze and knew her heart was telling the truth. His first thought was to grant her forgiveness, but something caught in his spirit. Amanda was wrong, but so was he. They had both spent so much time on everyone and everything else, they didn't see their own marriage fracturing and falling apart. He had been too busy to care. In that moment he decided things would be different. He would be different. So, instead he responded, "Me too."

They kissed. He immediately began to feel all that he had felt the first time they kissed. Like a breath of fresh air their marriage seemed renewed.

Amanda and Donny talked for a long time, and while they clearly weren't finished when they went to bed, they were moving in a new direction.

The next morning, Donny woke up early and texted Scott about breakfast and they met at the usual spot. Donny left a note for Amanda on the way out, telling her they still needed to talk, but together they would figure it all out.

When they got their food ordered, Scott asked, "So, what happened?"

"Honestly, I am not completely sure. I went in. I heard you telling me to race, so I did. We hugged, we cried, we kissed, we talked, we slept."

"Good start."

"I feel refreshed," Donny admitted. "Free."

"Forgiveness will do that," Scott said, "but you experienced a powerful piece of what makes healing quicker. When you are offended, particularly when someone is repentant, we must not hesitate. We must race to forgive.

You know the story of the Prodigal Son?"

"Yes," Donny said.

"What did the Father do when the son returned home?"

"He ran to him."

"Yes!" Scott was emphatic. "And you see, it was not only healing for Amanda, it was healing for you as well. When we wait to forgive others, it hurts us. It extends the separation and pain. Also, it slows the healing process when repentance does happen, because trust is harder to reestablish when we hesitate to forgive those who hurt us."

Scott pulled a napkin out of his pocket, and Donny knew it was one he had been given last night.

Scott smiled and began. Here is the secret:

1. Recognize our own brokenness.

   Do you remember me telling you about the actor Chris Pratt giving an acceptance speech at the Mtv awards? Another thing he said was, 'Nobody is perfect. People are gonna tell you 'You're perfect just the way you are.' You're not! You are imperfect. You always will be, but there is a powerful force that designed you that way, and if you're willing to accept that you will have grace."

   Jesus tells the story of the unforgiving servant, who learned that when we don't forgive as we have been forgiven, we lose.

   When we start by recognizing our own brokenness we are ready to forgive others, before they even sin.

2. Accept the pre-payment.

   If you accept Jesus as savior, and you believe that Jesus' sacrifice was truly once for all, then you believe that He has paid the price for the sins others commit against you. This gets complicated, and is hard to live out, but it is so important to our ability to live graciously. It is what holds relationships together and even makes them thrive even though we as people are broken.

   When we accept Jesus sacrifice on our own behalf, we also accept on behalf of everyone else. This means His death is enough payment to you for the sins committed against you.

   Are you with me?" Scott looked up.

"I think so," Donny said. "That's huge."
"Yes, it is. It is everything," Scott continued,

3. Cancel the debt.

   This is the hard part of forgiveness. Even when we agree that the penalty is paid, we still must not hold people to a new standard based on their failure. The struggle is we still should hold high standards, and expect people to pursue a godly standard, but not so that we don't get hurt, but so that they don't. This is why forgiveness is a daily choice. Every day for the rest of your lives, you must release Amanda from the penalty of her offense. It will get easier, but at some point, your enemy will bring back up, and you have to acknowledge again, the debt is paid.

"What if someone keeps committing the same offense?" Donny asked.
"You will need to answer 3 questions:

1. Is Jesus blood enough?

2. How many times did Jesus say to forgive your brother?

3. Is continuing this relationship in its current form good for the other person?

Too many people believe that forgiveness necessitates a relationship remaining the same. Often times, this is not true, but if I believe in human dignity and that one has to make their own decisions, then I will give them choice, and accept their decision. 'If you continue in your current practice, the consequence will be _____." If they opted to continue, they have made their choice. You did not.

4. Encourage signs of change.

    If you remember our TRAPPED teaching, you know that some idolatry becomes entrenched, and it can be hard to give up your gods, even when they are false. Therefore, whenever you see signs of growth or change, acknowledge them, embrace them, celebrate them. That is what forgiveness looks like.

"Wow, Scott, I am spinning," Donny admitted as he looked over the napkin. "The last 24 hours have been a whirlwind."

"Yes, I will be praying for you. Can you do me a favor?"

"Sure."

"Rest. All this emotion will cause you to crash if you don't stop on purpose."

"You got it."

Donny and Scott said their good-byes, and Donny picked up the tab.

He went home and spent the day with his family. Sharing what he had learned with Amanda. Together they enjoyed the first family day they had had in a long time.

CHOOSE INTEGRITY

Over the next several weeks Donny's home became renewed in so many ways. He and Amanda felt like honeymooners, and the girls seemed to be thriving in the love of their parents. At work, turning the corner with his teams, had taken more time than Donny thought it should, but he was keeping a hard line on the budget. Scott was at karate a few times, but Jeff did most of the teaching. Thursday breakfast was hit or miss depending on Scott's treatment.

One Thursday when Scott was unable to meet, Donny went into the office early. Breakfast at the diner just wasn't the same without Scott these days. So, Donny picked up a fast-food sausage with egg biscuit and headed into the office. A few security people and some maintenance workers were around, but mostly the place was quiet.

When Donny arrived at his office, he immediately got to work. He opened the current social media marketing plan and began reviewing various campaigns.

The wonder of Facebook and other social media was the value. The company achieved so much reach for so little money. Scott opened the analytics file and began scrolling through each post to see if a pattern could be found as to which posts were the most effective. The plan was to find the effective material and focus resources on those types of posts.

Donny used his laptop to put numbers into a spreadsheet that counted reach vs. engagement and gave each post a score. To keep from flipping back and forth between apps, Donny used his phone to scroll through the posts. When unexpectedly Donny received a message request from a girl he didn't know, but the girl's lack of clothes and the look in her eye stirred temptation in Donny. He deleted it and went back to work. Her eyes and cleavage kept popping back into Donny's mind. His curiosity started to play in his imagination.

Donny knew he loved Amanda and she loved him. At the moment, his heart was full, and he and Amanda were having plenty of sex, but his mind still played. What would it be like with another woman? Would different be good? He wasn't actually going to have sex with someone else, he was just wondering about how to spice up his own sex life with Amanda. Looking would be research.

"Stop!" For a moment Donny was afraid he had screamed out loud, but it was only a thought. He needed help. He couldn't seem to stop himself from running down these sexual rabbit trails. How does a man remain pure, when his mind is drawn so easily to sex?

Donny stood up and walked over to the window and stared out praying, "God, help me to be pure. Help me to fight this thing inside of me that longs to look at other women. I love Amanda, but sex has become an addiction. No, it runs deeper than that it is . . ." Donny searched his thoughts for the word, "an idol."

"It can be hard to give up your gods." Donny heard Scott say again. When Scott had said it, Donny had thought only about Amanda's struggle, he had not thought about his own idols. Then he began to wonder how much Amanda was hurting, having given up her contact with Braydon. Then he wondered if she had given it up.

Remembering that he had been praying, Donny stopped, "Help me, Lord, just help."

As he shared lunch with John, Donny kept getting distracted by the thought of Amanda being tempted to reengage with Braydon. At one point, John noticed, and asked, "You seem distracted today? Are you ok?"

Donny was a little taken back, as these meetings were almost always strictly business. Donny heard Scott in his head, "Honesty shines light into the world." So, he told the truth, "Well, John, Amanda and I have been having issues for some time. We got help, and things seem to be better the last few weeks. They are better. But today I am having doubts, and I can't seem to focus on work without worrying."

John looked uncomfortable, and Donny wondered if he had just overstepped the lines by getting personal. Finally, John pulled his cell phone out of his desk drawer and set a timer. Donny was puzzled.

"Ok, we are going to take a break for 10 minutes, no more," and John pushed start. "Donny, I don't know much about your home life, but can I give you advise?"

"Sure," Donny didn't know what a divorced man could say to help, but he had gotten used to being teachable.

"When I got divorced, it wasn't the obvious stuff that destroyed us. It was the questions I didn't ask. My wife and I had been pulling away from each other for more than a year, and I never once asked myself why. I made up every reason on my own, but it was never my fault. In my head, I rationalized the problems away. Then I found out she had been having an affair for nine of the twelve months that we had been having big issues."

John leaned forward on his elbows and took his glasses off, "Donny, if you have concerns, you have to ask the tough questions, especially if your marriage has any chance of recovery. It's not the things that everyone sees that destroy us, it is who we are when no one is looking."

Donny suddenly was thinking less about Amanda than his own struggle with pornography. "What were you hiding?" Donny didn't know that John had hidden anything and wasn't completely sure why he had asked the question.

John looked shocked for a minute, then softened, "Donny, that is not a question we like to answer as men, is it?" John waited for Donny to answer, but Donny just sat as if it were a rhetorical question. "You're right though, it wasn't all her. Donny, I drank and would spend my evenings out with guys from here at clubs, often we were at strip clubs. I figured I brought home enough money and influence for Carol and the kids to be fine. I didn't realize the value of being there."

Donny thought about Ray, he had said John used to hang out with them.

"When Carol left, she just left a note and disappeared. Now, I am the only one available for my kids. Carol calls from time to time, and the kids miss her, but she's kind of a mess. I think she doesn't want to see the kids again until she figures herself out.

I admit she did me a favor. I needed clarity. I had lost focus on what was important in life. When Carol left, I looked at the broken-hearted faces of my kids and knew it had to change. So, I quit staying after hours, started working through lunch, so I could be at home at night, and made my kids my everything."

"What about the drinking?" Donny felt something stirring, but he wasn't sure what it was.

"Well, all this is hard. I still drink after the kids go to bed, but I am not sure I could get through without it." John's honesty was refreshing and concerning.

Donny thought for a moment about his next question, "Do you go to church?"

John got a stern look on his face then softened again, "You just keep digging where it hurts don't you?"

"John, I figure we're in this deep, I might as well help if I can."

"I thought I was helping you," John said. Then, "I keep thinking about it, but I have so much guilt, I am not sure I could take anymore. I worry about the kids though."

Donny understood John's hesitation, then in a moment of inspiration he asked, "What about martial arts?"

John looked puzzled, so Donny kept going, "I have a friend who teaches martial arts, and we get a lesson every week about living life. The lessons also teach us about God's ways." Donny thought about his invitation and felt a little guilty about not sticking with the church invite, but continued, "I go with my kids every week. It's good family time."

"Wow, I never thought about it before. Maybe . . ." John's alarm went off. "Well, saved by the bell. Time to get back to work. That wasn't too bad." John stood up and put out his hand. Donny realized, he was serious about cutting off the conversation. Donny was shocked by the abruptness, but he stood, shook John's hand and headed back to his office.

As he walked, he thought through the conversation. He needed to talk to Amanda tonight. He didn't want to mess up what seemed so good right now, but he didn't want secrets to kill their marriage either. John's admissions and openness were refreshing. He even had to admit, that John's clarity at the end, though unexpected, was also refreshing. The whole conversation was a light. "Honesty," he thought, "always shines light." When he got to his office, he called Scott.

"Hey Donny." Scott answered with his usual cheer.

"Hey Scott, how are you?" Donny genuinely wanted to know and didn't want to dive in too quickly to his own needs.

"I'm doing ok today. I usually struggle the day of and the day after chemo. But give me a day or two, and I am right as rain."

"Awesome. So glad to hear it. I miss you, man. What are the doctors telling you?"

"Donny, they are telling me everything is working the way it should, but then I already knew that." Scott had gotten serious, and Donny was used to the teacher coming out in Scott. "What's up with you, my friend?"

"I am good. Amanda and I are really starting to find ourselves again. Thank you."

"Awesome. Did you call just to check in?"

"Actually, no, but I don't want to take advantage of you either." Donny started to feel guilty for calling.

"Donny, I am bored out of my mind. Please, let me help."

"Ok," Donny dove in head first to the deep end. "I have been struggling today with the temptation to look at pornography."

"Have you looked?"

"No, but I keep thinking about it." Donny relayed the story of the pop-up message, and his internal battle. "I had a truly personal conversation with John Cauley, and it was interesting to hear his thoughts. He said when he got divorced it was the unknown that destroyed his marriage."

"Sounds about right," Scott responded. "Donny, the most important stuff is who we are when no one is looking." The fact that Scott had just quoted John was a little surprising to Donny, and yet, it made that phrase stick. "What happens behind closed doors is far more vital than what happens in public, and what happens in public is guided by what happens behind closed doors."

"John said something similar," Donny admitted.

"I may have to meet this John," Scott joked.

"I did invite him to martial arts," Donny said.

"Great! Let's not get off track though. Donny, I am so glad you called, because John is right, and you should get help when temptation is crouching at your door. The numbers vary, from the high sixties to the low eighties, but the percentage of Christian men struggling with this sin is appalling. Worse still is the unwillingness for most men to discuss it openly. Whether it is embarrassment, guilt or a combination, I am not sure. What I am sure of is that sin in darkness has power.

Donny, I am also sure that this sin could destroy everything you have started to rebuild."

"That's my fear," Donny admitted.

"Listen to me, Brother, Integrity is one of the most important choices you can make to sustain thriving relationships. Now most people don't understand what that means, because they equate integrity and honesty. While honesty is a part of integrity, integrity literally means single-mindedness. True integrity has three components: Clarity, consistency, and character. Where these components line up, we have confidence in each other. Whenever they are off, we struggle to trust."

There was a pause on the line, so Donny said, "I'm with you."

"Good, but I decided to write these down to give to you later.

First, we need clarity. Have you ever noticed how easy it is to deal with a person, you don't like, when they are clear about their agenda? When we set clear standards for ourselves and live a life that is guided by that clarity, people feel safer around us. They may not agree with us, but they know the rules we play by, and so they can hold to those rules. I heard someone say something to the effect of 'The cruelest thing a leader can do is to be unclear.' That may not be exact, but it is the gist."

Donny thought about how John's clarity had made him feel better about their conversation. He trusted John more, because he was clear, even though John had ended their talk abruptly.

"Second, we need consistency. Donny, particularly right now, as you are just getting your bearings again with Amanda, consistency is a key to keeping momentum. Any time we have had a fractured relationship, we need to make changes, and then prove over time that we can hold to those changes."

"What if someone isn't consistent?" Donny asked.

"Well, it makes trust hard to rebuild."

"What if they are trying, but as you said, 'It is hard to give up our gods.'?"

"What are you getting at, Donny?"

"What if Amanda is still in touch with Braydon? What should I do?"

"Donny, it depends. If you are expecting Amanda to not struggle, you are fooling yourself, but if you are worried, she is lying about her desire to cut Braydon off, then there is a trust issue. Which proves my point."

"I don't think she is lying, but I know how much I struggle with temptation to go back to my old gods, so I have been wondering about her."

"Ok Donny," Scott took a breath, "I need to be clear, so listen carefully. Talk to Amanda!" Scott almost shouted into the phone.

Donny heard John again.

"What stays in the dark has power. If you talk to Amanda, and she is struggling (just like you). Race to forgive her. If she is not struggling, because she really has moved on, then your fears will be relieved. Celebrate. If she is not struggling, because she is not trying to stop, then you know your problems still exist. Address them.

You should not expect perfection but encourage any growth. Most importantly, get it all in the open. Over time consistency regrows trust, but it takes time and openness.

Last, we need to align our character. Again, integrity and character are often used interchangeably, but character is only a part of integrity. Still, it is the core part. Character is, as John said, 'Who you are when no one is looking.'

Character is the part of who we are that will remain when everything else burns. It is our level of fortitude and will. Character is determined in the prayer closet, not the public square, but nothing happens in public that is unaffected by our character. It is why men like Hitler can gain power and yet we know they are evil. Hitler was a man of single-minded focus. He was clear in his agenda, consistent in his direction, and had fortitude and will. What bothers us, is that his character was flawed. The difference between a hero and a villain is character. Both have it, but one is good, and one is bad.

When our clarity of focus, consistency in direction, and good character are aligned, we have true integrity. The strength of all of that plays out in our lives."

"Wow, that's good stuff as always, Scott."

"Well, thanks, but you know this is all God."

"I do, but thanks for letting him speak through you."

"Donny, I will be praying for you."

"Thanks, Scott."

As Donny hung up the phone, he thought through his conversation with both John and Scott and decided that a date night with Amanda was in order. So, he called her to "ask her out". They made plans for Friday night. Amanda sounded excited. Then the conversation was interrupted by a knock at the door. Greg Mullins, a director from another department stuck his head in the door. Donny waved him in and said his goodbyes to Amanda.

"Hey Greg, what's up?" Greg had never come into Donny's office for a meeting, and he didn't look happy.

"Donny, I need to tell you something, and I am not here to gossip, but feel you need to know. I also need you to keep this confidential. Can I count on you?" Greg sounded very official. Donny just nodded and worried.

"We have been doing an audit over the last few months and found some unexpected discrepancies. I couldn't figure out where we were losing money, so I have been doing my own quiet, but deep investigation.

Donny, Ray has been embezzling from the company for some time now. It took us a long time to find it, because he has been writing the reports.

I know he is your friend, and I know the rumor mill can get crazy, so before all of this becomes public, I wanted you to know the whole truth."

Donny sat stunned; unsure how to respond. Greg turned and walked out the door. A few minutes later, Donny saw Ray being marched out of the building by security. He wanted to check on his friend, but he also was too shocked to know how to respond. The value of integrity hit home like a hammer hitting an anvil.

"Thank you, Jesus, for protecting me from myself today." Donny prayed, turned back to his computer, and just stared.

The next evening Donny and Amanda headed for dinner, on the way to the restaurant the conversation lulled, and Donny considered asking her about Braydon. Fear took over, and he just drove instead. Amanda noticed something was off, so she asked, "Are you ok?"

"I have a lot on my mind," Donny's fear made him hesitate, but he needed to know what was happening with his wife. "Did I tell you about Ray?"

"Yes. Honey, I am so sorry. I know he has been your friend for a long time. Have you talked to him?"

Donny suddenly felt a pang of guilt. He had been so caught up in his own worries, he hadn't called Ray. "No, I've been a little distracted. I should call."

"By what?"

Donny was quiet.

"Honey? Distracted by what?" Amanda insisted.

"Character." Donny's fear continued to gnaw at the edges of his conscience.

"What?!" Clearly Amanda was lost by Donny's evasive response.

Donny decided it was time, but he still ambled his way to his burning question. He told Amanda about the pop-up, she was obviously concerned by it. He assured her that he had not looked. He told her about his conversations with John and Scott but left out the details surrounding Braydon. He explained Scott's integrity framework, as best he could remember it. Above all he remembered that character is who you are when no one is looking. Then, he risked the evening, "I'm worried about Braydon still."

Amanda was slow to respond, "What are you worried about?"

Donny got nervous, "I know how easily I am tempted to go back to my old ways. I know you said you were stopping, but I worry that you will be tempted to keep things up with Braydon, and just keep it hidden."

They both rode quietly for a minute or two.

"Are you still emailing him?" Donny finally asked the burning question and felt he had left accusation out of his voice.

"No," Amanda answered, "but he has emailed me a few times." Amanda was quiet and clearly saddened. "I have wanted to send him a quick note to tell him, "It is over," but I am scared I won't stop. Honestly, I am scared to be alone if you and I can't keep this marriage working."

Donny was stunned that Amanda was worried their marriage might not work. The fact that she was keeping her options open stung. How would they ever get whole if she was holding on to Braydon?

"Amanda, I don't think we can survive unless we are both all in, forever."

Tears formed in Amanda's eyes. "Can you forgive me?"

"Race!" Donny heard Scott again.

"Yes," Donny answered softly, "but you have to cut it off."

"I know, but I am scared he will just draw me back in."

Donny wasn't sure what to do. Amanda was trying, but the ties weren't broken. How would they heal if she didn't cut Braydon off? As they pulled into the parking lot of the restaurant, they were both obviously overwhelmed. Donny parked, and they just sat. Finally, he turned to Amanda and looked her in the eye. "If you really want this, we will figure it out . . . together."

Amanda smiled through her tears, leaned in and kissed Donny in a way that gave him hope.

BEDROCK

CHOOSE SUBMISSION

Donny and Amanda were able to get through dinner with minimal disruption. A few moments of silence, but then one of them would turn to small talk again. They were both trying hard to keep the night pleasant. As Donny finished paying the check, his phone rang. He would normally check it to make sure it wasn't the girls, then leave it if it wasn't, but it was Scott. He showed the screen to Amanda to get permission before answering, and Amanda nodded.

"Hey Scott!" Donny answered.

"Hey Donny, it's Kathy."

Donny was immediately concerned. Kathy had never called him, and she was on Scott's phone.

"We don't want you to worry," Kathy said, as if those words ever worked, "but Scott wanted me to call and ask for your prayers. He started feeling extra sick today, and the doctor's have admitted him for more tests. We will probably be here all weekend for observation and wanted to see if you guys would check in on the girls."

Donny's face had grown more and more concerned as he listened, and Amanda began mouthing the words, "What's wrong?"

Donny tried to listen and see Amanda at the same time. He felt distracted and overwhelmed. So, he simply held up his finger for Amanda to wait. She seemed put off, but he needed to listen.

"We would be happy to check on the girls. Is there anything you guys need while you're there?"

"No, we are ok," Kathy assured him.

"Ok, we will check back in tomorrow." Donny hung up and stood up. "Scott's in the hospital, and Kathy wants us to check in on the girls."

"Oh my goodness," Amanda said, "What's going on?"

"They don't know anything yet. They are running some tests." Donny felt a bit annoyed, Amanda had heard how short the conversation was.

"What happened?" Amanda also seemed annoyed. Donny just wanted to get out of the restaurant without a scene.

"I'll tell you everything in the car," he said.

Once in the car Donny gave Amanda the few details she didn't already have. Amanda seemed frustrated that he didn't know more. "You have to ask more questions?" Amanda half joked.

"I was trying to be respectful of their time." Donny's voice raised a little.

"So, what are we doing?" Amanda asked.

"I thought we would check on the girls."

"Who's girls?"

"Scott and Kathy's girls." Donny thought this was obvious.

"You could have meant our girls." Amanda's voice came up as well.

Suddenly, Donny was struck by how easily a simple misunderstanding could turn sour so quick. "I'm sorry," he said. "I'm just worried."

"I know," Amanda quieted. She reached over and grabbed his hand and squeezed. "Do you think we should call ahead?"

"I only have Scott's number," Donny said.

"I have Alex's," Amanda said and began to dial.

Donny half listened as he drove, and his mind spun. Stress can bring on a fight in just a few minutes. Somehow Amanda had to break off her ties to Braydon but was afraid. Alex seemed to have things under control. How were they supposed to make it, if they couldn't keep from fighting over silly things? Was Scott going to die? How would he respond to losing Scott? Should he call Ray tomorrow?

"Donny!" Amanda was almost shouting.

"What?!"

"Alex said she thinks they are fine for tonight. We can probably wait until tomorrow to check in."

"Ok," Donny answered, and Amanda said goodbye to Alex.

"Where did you go?" It sounded like an accusation.

"What are you talking about?" Donny felt defensive.

"I was trying to talk to you, and you weren't hearing me."

"I was thinking about other things." Donny could hear his voice was raised, but he couldn't seem to calm down. How could Amanda be upset with him for just thinking? "You were talking to Alex, so my mind wandered."

"Where?" Amanda's voice was a mix of frustration and shock.

"To our small fight at the end of dinner, then Braydon, then Scott, then Ray," with each new thought Donny's voice got louder.

"Why are you yelling at me?"

"Seriously," Donny thought. "You've basically just accused me of being a bad listener, because I wasn't focused on your conversation with someone else." Out loud he said, "I'm just a *little* overwhelmed."

They rode in silence for a moment, and Donny's mind began to wander again. He didn't want to be mad at Amanda, but his emotions were in turmoil. The last twenty-four hours had been some of the most confusing of his life.

"I'm sorry," Amanda said.

"Me too," Donny answered. He took his turn to reach over and squeeze Amanda's hand.

The next few days were a whirlwind, between checking on the Roland girls and keeping up with their own, Donny and Amanda were exhausted on Sunday after lunch with all 6 girls together, so they took a nap. They woke up to the sound of Donny's phone ringing. The caller ID said "Scott".

"Hello," Donny answered.

"Hey Donny," it was good to hear Scott's voice on the other end of the line. "I wanted to give you an update and thank you for helping with the girls."

"Any time, Scott," Donny answered, but wondered if he could really do this anytime for Scott. He was still exhausted.

"Listen, Kathy is going to go home tonight and stay with the girls. It looks like I might have to stay here a while."

"Wow, I'm sorry Scott. What are they telling you?"

"Well, the chemo has just weakened my immune system, and they want to keep me in a more sterile environment. It looks like it could be a few weeks, but we really don't know."

"Ok. What can we do?"

"Nothing for now. I thought I would see if you want to make the trip over for breakfast one day this week."

"How's Tuesday sound?"

"Sounds great, see you then." Scott hung up the phone. Donny turned to Amanda and filled her in.

"Those poor girls," was all she got out, before she started crying.

Donny didn't know what to do, so he held her for a little bit. Then got up to check on his own daughters and fix dinner.

By the time Tuesday morning rolled around, Donny struggled to get out of bed too make the early morning journey to Scott's hospital room. The past week had left him wrung out. Yesterday, had been a whirlwind at work, and he had finally talked to Ray. Ray had spent most of the time explaining why he did what he did, and from Donny's perspective, it sounded like Ray thought the company owed him what he had taken. Donny was shocked at his friend's lack of repentance or even contrition. Ray was most upset that he had been caught. Donny knew from the Monday meetings that the company was planning to press charges but ask for restoration and probation as a kindness to Ray. By the time Donny, found Scott's room, he was already overwhelmed at what lay ahead.

He knocked.

"Come in," Scott sounded almost cheerful.

"Hey Scott," Donny said as he walked in.

"Donny, how are you?"

Donny paused and considered his answer. "I'm exhausted Scott. This last week has really been tough emotionally, spiritually, and physically. I can't seem to slow down anything, and I can't seem to keep up either. I know I shouldn't complain, my life is full and getting better, but I'm just struggling to find rest." Donny immediately felt guilty for spilling his guts to the man with cancer lying in a hospital bed.

"Wow, you've come a long way, my friend." Scott said almost proud.

Donny stared back puzzled by his mentors response.

"When we first started this journey together, you were hiding behind the standard masks. Now look at you, spilling the whole truth without reservation."

"Sorry," Donny said.

"Don't be. Relationships grow when we choose vulnerability. They grow through awareness. If you aren't safe enough to be honest with me, then we haven't become as close as I thought."

"I trust you. I just hate to add to your load. You have enough to worry about."

"Donny, Donny, Donny," Scott said in a patronizing voice, "We share our burdens and they all get lighter. I can't tell you what a comfort it was to call on you to check on the girls and know you did so immediately. We are in this life together. Sharing each other's burdens is what makes life worth living."

"Ok, ok," Donny said, "So what are the doctors saying since Sunday."

"Not much, they are going to run some more blood tests this afternoon, but they expect at least a week of observation." Scott paused, "Can I tell you the worst part?"

"Sure, we share burdens," Donny's voice and smile expressed his jibe.

"I'm bored out of my mind. Thank you so much for coming."

"Sure," Donny really was happy to just sit with his friend.

"So?" Scott prodded.

"So, what?" Donny responded.

"Catch me up on Donny." Scott was insistent.

"Well, let's see . . . You know about my conversation with John Cauley. Did I tell you about Ray?"

"No."

"He's been embezzling from the company. They told me after we talked on Thursday."

"This is your friend, who helped you get your job?" Scott checked.

"Yes."

"How's that working for you?"

"It's weird mostly. I know we've been friends a long time, but there has been a growing distance between us lately, now this. Then when I talked to him last night, he actually blamed the company for taking advantage of him. I don't know what to think."

"How's it going for you at work?" Scott asked.

"It's fine." Donny didn't think anything about Ray's decisions affecting him until just now. "Honestly, Scott, I haven't thought twice about how this affects me. I am just going to keep working as hard as I always have."

Scott smiled.

"What?" Donny asked.

"You didn't think about you. I'm so proud I could bust. Donny, so many people in your position would be thinking only about how this would affect them. You have just kept being you and working with integrity. Keep it up, and I bet you go far."

"Thanks," Donny said, "I think."

"What about you and Amanda?"

"Well, she hasn't emailed Braydon, but he has emailed her. She says she doesn't know how to write the note to cut it off, and she is afraid of how he will respond. She is also afraid of letting go of him, in case things don't work out with us." Donny decided not to add his own commentary to get Scott's unobstructed response.

"Sounds like you still have some work to do," was all Scott said.

"Yeah, it hurts that she isn't sure about us, but I guess I am just scared about her keeping these lines open. I told her I understood the struggle to let go. I just don't know what else to do."

"Break it off for her."

"What? Me? You think I should try talking to this guy?" Offense oozed from Donny.

"Donny, do you love Amanda?"

"Yes." This wasn't helping ease Donny's frustration.

"Would you give anything for her to be the woman God made her to be?"

"Yes." Donny sensed a trap.

"Would you die for her?"

"Yes." Where was this going?

"Then call Braydon and tell him, 'It is over.'"

"You can't be serious." Now Donny's offense was complete. "This is her fault, her responsibility. Why should I be the one fixing anything?"

"Do you love her?"

"I do, but I didn't start all this. This is not my fault!" Donny was emphatic.

Scott's voice kept getting softer, "Why did Jesus die?"

Totally defensive, Donny almost yelled, "I am not God!"

"No, you are not. Which means you are not perfect. You are not without sin. You can't save your wife from eternal condemnation, but you can save her from Braydon. You can be her advocate, her mediator.

'Husbands love your wives as Christ loved the Church and gave himself up for her.'"

Suddenly, Donny understood. All this time, he had read over that verse with a weak understanding of love. Christ didn't just die for our sins, he suffered and died. Before that he gave up heaven and became one of us. How much did Christ love us?

Scott saw the wheels turning, so he pressed in, "Donny, this is the seventh and most important choice. It is the bedrock of all thriving relationships. We must choose submission."

Donny just sat, listening but buzzing. His mind was turning over everything he was going through, every-thing that had changed. He thought about John, Ray, the girls, Amanda, his friendship with Scott, his anger toward Braydon, his own sin, his own forgiveness. He saw visions of Christ crucified from watching movies. He thought about what he knew about Christ's suffer-ing. He knew Scott was speaking truth, but everything in him wanted to fight it.

In the quiet he heard a whisper, "Will you love her like I do?" It wasn't Scott, he looked at him to check. It was the first time he thought he heard the voice of God. Maybe it was just his own mind, but the words were too deep too real. Donny began to weep.

Scott waited patiently, never saying a word.

When Donny finally got control of himself he said, "I don't know if I can."

"You will need help, but you are never alone." Scott answered.

"Scott, how do I do this? What if I fail her again? What if I fail Jesus? How do I keep myself from mess-ing everything up? I know I haven't stolen from my company, but I also know I am just as selfish as Ray was. Scott, what am I going to do?"

"Donny, we all fail. Every day is a battle between being self-focused or God focused. When we understand the battle, we can choose against it, but it starts with submission." Scott paused. "Are you up for a little coaching?" Scott asked.

"Please," Donny knew he needed help, he knew there was so much more to learn form Scott, he prayed God would give them more time.

Scott turned to his bed side table, opened the drawer, and pulled out a pen and napkin. "Tell Amanda, 'Thank you.' I have been handing out napkins since Saturday morning."

At the top of the napkin Scott wrote SUBMISSION in big letters.

"First let's give a definition:

> Submission is a chosen heart-set not just a mindset, to surrender one's will, plans, wants, needs, agendas, dreams, and even one's life for the sake of another.

Two keys to catch here:

1. Submission that creates, builds, and sustains thriving productive relationships must be a choice. It cannot be forced.

2. Submission is a matter of the heart. It is the why behind our choices. People can do the submissive act, and not be submissive.

The struggle I face so often in teaching on this choice, is that we either want to lessen the severity of the meaning of submission, or we want to argue that it only works when both people do it. We all struggle daily to live in submission, but when we do, submission has powerful ramifications. Submission is the choice to love, the freedom to live, and the power to lead.

Most of us struggle, because the image of submission seems weak. In fact, the word literally means 'under the feet of.' The picture painted by the word is of you lying on the ground with someone's foot on your neck and their sword at your throat. Not comfortable." Scott looked up to make sure Donny was with him.

"I'm already not sure I like where this is going," Donny admitted.

"Yeah, but here's the thing, Jesus turns the whole thing on it's head. Jesus showed us that the truly powerful one is not the one with the sword!

Jesus is clearly more powerful than you or I, right?"

"Sure," Donny answered.

"Jesus can, God can, at any moment force us into a position of submission. Yet, though he rules everything, he chooses to give us his sword, and lay down, putting our feet on his neck and his sword at his own throat, and let's us decide what to do." Scott could see the lights coming on for Donny, "In the kingdom of God, the strong choose to submit for the sake of the weak, and everybody wins. When you choose to submit, you choose the position of the strong."

Donny sat back in his chair, the paradigm shifts in his head were massive. "So, laying my life down for another gives me more power in the relationship."

"Every time," Scott confirmed.

"But what if only one person submits, isn't the other one just committing abuse?"

"To an extent, yes."

"So, what do you do, I mean you aren't suggesting people stay in an abusive relationship are you?"

Donny's defenses were going up again. His best friend growing up had been abused.

"Well, it depends." Scott said, and Donny was ready to fight back, "If the abuse has grown to the point of physical harm, it is in the best interest of everyone, even and especially the abuser, for the abused to take a stand for their safety and get out. Even when the abuse is constant emotional abuse, there may be a place for leaving that is best for everyone.

Donny, this is where this gets difficult. Where do you draw the lines? The problem is that every person is unique, and the lines need to be drawn by them. Submission is your choice. The other difficulty is that this is a heart choice. You can leave an abuser for their sake. That is still submissive. When you choose submission, you are choosing to put someone else's interest ahead of your own."

Scott could see that Donny was trying to process so he waited.

"So, you're saying submission is being self-less?" Donny posed the statement as a question.

"Well, sort of. I'm saying that true submission is keeping yourself out of the center. You see, there are times we need to choose things to take care of ourselves for the sake of others. This can be as simple as choosing to take time away from family, friends, and work to exercise, or as deep as severing a relationship for the other persons benefit. The act may seem selfish, but because the heart is right, it is in fact an act of submission." Scott saw that Donny was getting overwhelmed, "I know this is complicated. There are volumes written on this one idea."

"It is a lot to take in, but how can I choose it if I don't understand it?" Donny asked.

"Well, let me show you this way." Scott turned the napkin over. "There are ten ways we try to take God's place:

1. Set standards for others. Instead of giving others the dignity to be a part of setting standards, we decide how they should think, act, respond, etc.

2. Expect adherence to our standards. Not only do we judge people when they react in a way that is contrary to what we think they should do, we expect them to think and act like us. If we are "on time" people, we expect everyone else to be "on time" and judge them if they are not.

   You can see how these choices are really choices that only God can make.

3. Look for acceptance, appreciation, and attention from others. We almost daily look to others to give us value; however, the word we use for giving worth to someone is worship. Can you see the problem?"

Scott continued,

4. Fault-Finding." Scott wrote these two words stacked on top of each other. "It is not our job to point out to others what is wrong with them. We should look to praise them. If they ask for our help in seeing blind spots, then we can step in, but when we make a practice of finding fault and criticizing others, we express arrogance that somehow, we are better than others, and, of course, we are not.

5. Others become totally my responsibility. The word "totally" is important. We do have a responsibility to help each other through life, but when I begin to believe that your decisions are my responsibility, I rob you of dignity and God of his place.

6. Controlling of circumstance and people. Whenever we try to control other's decisions or our circumstances we fool ourselves. You can't even decide if you will be alive in the next moment, much less control anything beyond your own choices.

7. Unwilling to forgive. We have talked about forgiveness before, but this is a sure sign you are not being submissive. If you are unwilling to forgive others, you have decided you are better than they are.

8. Self-sufficiency or independence. When we try to live life without others, we set ourselves up for failure. Only God can exist without someone else.

9. Expect to always be right. Do I need to say more about this?" Scott looked up at Donny.

"No," Donny answered.

10. Defensiveness. Probably the quickest sign for me that I am being rebellious is that I get defensive. It makes me unable to learn, because I try to prove my stance is right. When someone challenges me, and I get defensive, I stand alone. As you can see this one position begins to influence so many of the others."

Donny thought about his own defensiveness earlier and began to wonder if Scott caught the connection. Scott started underlining the first letter of each choice, he underlined both "Fs" in fault-finding, and now Donny knew why he had stacked them. When Scott was done the letters spelled, SELF-FOCUSED.

"When we get self-focused we take God's place at the center of the universe," Scott said. "We try to form a world around us and our agenda. When we choose submission, we remove ourselves from the center and put God in his rightful place.

And here is the kicker: when we choose to give ourselves up for the sake of others, we become just like Jesus, and we gain the power to be loving and lead even when others abuse us."

"How do you trust someone who has taken advantage of your love?" Donny began to wonder if this was even possible.

"Well, we follow Jesus, who 'entrusted himself to him who judges justly.' Submission is not a matter of trusting others, it is a question of trusting God."

"So, you think I should stand up to Braydon, to protect Amanda, and leave the results in God's hand?" Donny needed to know how to live this choice out today!

"Yes," Scott said, "that is exactly what I think, but the choice is yours."

Donny suddenly thought to look at the clock. "Wow, I am gonna be late for work, Scott."

"Sorry," Scott was sincere.

Then just as sincerely Donny said, "Don't be. You have saved my marriage, and maybe me from years of struggle."

"Wow, that's pretty heavy," Scott tried not to be self-deprecating.

"I know, but your willingness to risk a breakfast, has changed everything for me." Donny started to choke up as he thought about Scott's fight for life. "I don't want you to die."

Scott smiled, "Don't write me off yet." They both laughed. "Thanks, though Donny, you have given me a reason to fight."

The two men hugged, Scott prayed, and Donny headed to work.

That night, Donny shared what Scott had shown him with Amanda. They sat together as Donny called Braydon. When Donny was done telling Braydon he was never to talk to Amanda again unless Donny was present, Braydon asked to speak with Amanda. Donny said, "No, move on. It's over."

When he hung up, Amanda wrapped Donny in a tight hug, and said, "Thank you."

That night they consummated their new direction with a life and joy, they had never experienced before.

On Thursday, all the Roland's and the East's met at the hospital where they shared dinner. The nurses coming in and out were surprised by the love in the room, and Donny got choked up when Scott introduced them as family.

Scott cried when Amanda pulled out a yellow manila folder and handed it to Scott. In it were all Scott's frameworks from all the napkins, typed and neatly put together in a small notebook. As the East family and the Roland children left the room together, there were still a lot of fears and questions around what would happen with Scott, but they all knew this was a night they would never forget.

EPILOGUE

Donny walked into the diner, and he saw Michael, a young man from the human resources department who had visited church the week before, sitting alone in a booth staring into his plate with a blank look on his face. He smiled. It had been two years since, Scott had found him in the exact same booth.

"A distracted man will often go hungry," he said.

Michael looked up surprised. "Hi, Mr. East."

"Call me, Donny. You alone?"

"Not if you join me."

Donny sat down as Sarah came to the table. "Coffee?" she asked.

"Yes, please. I'll also have my usual. And, Sarah, can I get some extra napkins?"

Sarah smiled knowingly as she walked away.

"So, Michael, what's got you so distracted you can't eat."

"Well, I'm not sure where to start," Michael said. "I just got this new job, Brittany is pregnant, and I can't seem to figure out how to stop fighting with her."

"Have you ever taken martial arts?" Donny asked.

"No," Michael had a quizzical look on his face.

"Well, for just over two years, I have been taking classes from one of my best friends. His name is Scott Roland. He goes to our church. He's taught me a lot about relationships and dealing with conflict. Maybe he could help you. If you're interested."

"I could use help," Michael said, "but I'm not sure about the martial arts."

"Understood," Donny answered, "Maybe I could help. If you want to take the risk."

"Honestly, Mr., I mean Donny, I would feel pretty vulnerable opening up to someone like you."

"Michael that's the first choice of every great relationship, vulnerability." Donny paused, then asked, "So, are you in?"

APPENDIX

7 Daily Choices

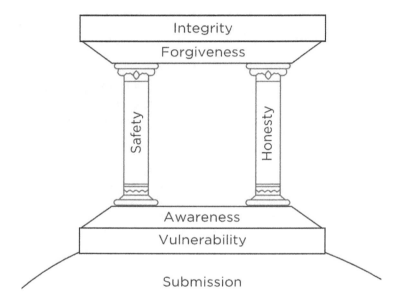

The Intimacy Triangle

"Our need for true intimacy is stronger than our need for food."

-Tim Buttrey of *True Relationships*

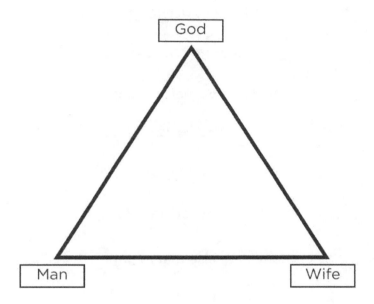

Vulnerability

Creating Thriving Productive Relationships

6-Step Apology

State the offense

Admit you were wrong

Apologize

Ask if they can forgive you

Ask for accountability

Ask for anything else that might be there

(Taylor 2017)

TRAPPED

Barriers Thriving Productive Relationships

6 Stages of Disease that Lead to the Death

Tired
↓
Raw
↓
Alone
↓
Pull-Away
↓
Private Sin
↓
Entrenched Sin
↓
Death

Awareness

Creating Thriving Productive Relationships

Mind Your Ps and Qs

Past Hurts

Present Struggles

Personality

Private Love Language

Quick to Listen

Question First

Quiet Your Answers

www.123test.com/disc-personality-test
www.5lovelanguages.com

Safety

Building Thriving Productive Relationships

A, E, I, O, U

Appreciate Differences

Encourage Strengths

"I" Language

Open Your Stance

Unlock Your History

Honesty

Building Thriving Productive Relationships

The Power of the Truth

Shines Light into the World

Hinders Self-Deception

Opens Us Up to Growth

Works Always

A Tale of Two Brains - https://www.youtube.com/watch?v=3XjUFYxSxDk

Chris Pratt MTV - https://www.youtube.com/watch?v=EihqXHqxri0

Forgiveness

Sustaining Thriving Productive Relationships

RACE to Forgive

Recognize Your Own Brokenness

Accept Pre-Payment

Cancel Debt

Encourage Signs of Change

Integrity

Sustaining Thriving Productive Relationships

3 Key Components of Integrity

Clarity

Consistency

Character

Submission

The Bedrock of Relationship

The Value of Submission

The Choice to Love

The Freedom to Live

The Power to Lead

Submission is a chosen heart-set not just a mindset, to surrender one's will, plans, wants, needs, agendas, dream, and even one's life for the sake of another.

SELF-FOCUSED

Set Expectations

Expect others to adhere to our standards

Look to others for acceptance, appreciation, and attention

Fault-Finding and criticism

Others become totally my responsibility

Controlling circumstances and people

Unwilling to Forgive

Self-sufficiency and independence

Expect to always be right

Defensive

The Great Example

Understanding Jesus:

1. Most Powerful Being in the Universe

2. Humbled Himself (Choose Vulnerability)

3. Walked in Our Shoes (Choose Awareness)

4. Came to Serve no to be Served (Choose Safety)

5. Was Truth (Choose Honesty)

6. One Mission (Choose Integrity)

7. Prayed for His Executioners (Choose Forgiveness)

8. Entrusted Himself to Him Who Judges Justly (Choose Submission)

9. Focused on Developing 12

10. Left with 120

11. 2000 years of Consistent Influence

12. Over 1 Billion Followers Today (Uncounted through the Years)

If you want to have a lasting impact, you need relationships that are thriving and productive.

If you want lasting influence and impact you must choose it.

BIBLIOGRAPHY

Adams, Marilee. 2004. *Change Your Questions/Change Your Life.* Berrett-Koehler Publishers.

Chapman, Gary. 2000. *The Five Love Languages: How to express Heartfelt Commitment to Your Mate.* Strand Publishing.

Covey, Stephen. 1989. *7 Habits of Highly Effective People.* Simon and Schuster.

Stanley, Andy. 2018. "I Owe Who." *Your Move podcast.* Atlanta, Georgia: Northpoint Ministries.

Taylor, Ford. 2017. *Relactional Leadership.* College Station, TX: High Bridge Books.

ABOUT THE AUTHOR

Dow Tippett was 11 years old when he first saw the Frank Capra classic "It's a Wonderful Life," and realized life is defined by relationships. For 30 years, Dow has taught couples and teams to live in healthy relationships that build influence and impact.

Now he brings his expertise to the marketplace by teaching, writing, and coaching leaders and teams in the workplace to be their very best and grow their productivity together.

He and his wife are raising their four daughters and pursuing a thriving life with each other.

Connect at: DowTippett.com or 7DailyChoices.com

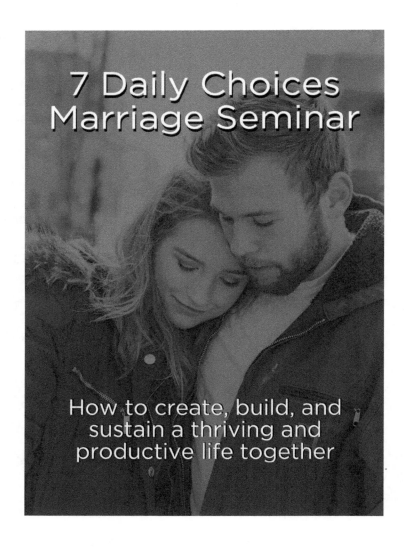

7 Daily Choices
Marriage Seminar

How to create, build, and
sustain a thriving and
productive life together

To host or join a 7 Daily Choices Marriage Seminar
near you or take the online course,
go to 7DailyChoices.com/Marriage.

7 Daily Choices
Leadership Seminar

How to create, build, and sustain a thriving and productive life with others

Contact us today for Corporate Leadership Seminars

7DailyChoices.com/Leadership

Bring Dow to Speak
at Your Event

Author. Speaker. Coach.

Dow understands the importance of choosing the right speaker for your event. The right one sets the stage for success, the wrong one for disaster. Dow's energetic, authentic approach combined with content that meets your needs, positions him as a top choice for businesses and non-profits alike. With over 30 years of speaking experience he customizes each event to your needs.